WADSWORTH PHILC

ON

KRIPKE

Consuelo Preti
College of New Jersey

THOMSON

WADSWORTH™

Australia • Canada • Mexico • Singapore • Spain • United Kingdom • United States

For more information about our products, contact us at:
Thomson Learning Academic Resource Center
1-800-423-0563

For permission to use material from this text, contact us by:
Phone: **1-800-730-2214**
Fax: **1-800-731-2215**
Web: **www.thomsonrights.com**

Asia
Thomson Learning
5 Shenton Way #01-01
UIC Building
Singapore 068808

Australia
Nelson Thomson Learning
102 Dodds Street
South Street
South Melbourne, Victoria 3205
Australia

Canada
Nelson Thomson Learning
1120 Birchmount Road
Toronto, Ontario M1K 5G4
Canada

Europe/Middle East/South Africa
Thomson Learning
High Holborn House
50-51 Bedford Row
London WC1R 4LR
United Kingdom

Latin America
Thomson Learning
Seneca, 53
Colonia Polanco
11560 Mexico D.F.
Mexico

Spain
Paraninfo Thomson Learning
Calle/Magallanes, 25
28015 Madrid, Spain

Preface
Acknowledgements

Preface

Saul Kripke is considered by many to be the most influential of all philosophers working on issues in mind and language in the 20th and 21st centuries. His work includes important and foundational theses in modal logic, a significant contribution to the theory of truth, an analysis of the semantic issues raised by translation, an interpretation of key issues in the work of Ludwig Wittgenstein, and, of course, the *Naming and Necessity* lectures, easily the most ground-breaking piece of philosophy written in the past 30 years.

This book offers a thorough, critical analysis and exposition of what are widely thought to be Kripke's most important contributions to philosophy: the semantics of modal logic; the issues raised in the *Naming and Necessity* lectures, and Kripke's interpretation of Wittgenstein. Commentary on Kripke's other work is also included.

This book is suitable for students of philosophy (both graduate and undergraduate), as well as for the non-specialist reader interested in contemporary philosophy of mind and language. The student of modal logic will find a general introduction to modal logic in Chapter 1. Critical commentary on the topics in Chapters 2 and 3 may be of interest to the scholar. The effort was made here to provide an accessible exposition of complex technical issues in logic, philosophy of language and the philosophy of mind to interested readers and students of philosophy, and to make the work of this monumental figure in contemporary philosophy available for the first time to a wider audience and from a wider perspective.

Acknowledgements

My thanks to the Guarino family, the Preti family, and Teresa Volpe (in Naples); and Michael Esposito and Tom Nolan (in New York), for making the circumstances of actually writing this book as pleasant as they could be.

Gary Ostertag read and commented on the manuscript in detail. Gary is a fierce and unremitting critic, and he has an impeccable eye for formal errors, solecisms, inelegant sentences, and places where I might have been said to be going out on a limb. I appreciate his hard work reading the drafts I sent him, and I am well aware that any errors left are my own.

Colin McGinn read the manuscript in draft and I thank him for his comments. I would also like to thank the anonymous referee for Wadsworth Publishers for his/her remarks. I am also very grateful to Saul Kripke for answering a number of my questions.

This book is dedicated to Annelyse Guarino Preti, my first teacher.

Consuelo Preti
New York City
September, 2002

1

Possible Worlds

Introduction

Saul Kripke is one of the few philosophers — and probably the only living philosopher — who has been called, with genuine merit, a genius.[1] He was a highly precocious child; even brilliant. In a feature article published in the *New York Times* in 1977, it is reported, for instance, that Kripke had read all of Shakespeare's work by age 10, and had taught himself geometry and calculus by age 14.[2] And, as a young teenager, he would travel to the library at the University of Nebraska at Lincoln, 60 miles from his home in Omaha, because the library there had materials important to his research that he couldn't get closer to home — like the *Journal of Symbolic Logic.*[3]

Saul Kripke doesn't have a Ph.D. in mathematics or philosophy — just a BA in Math from Harvard. He was, however, before his retirement, McCosh Professor of Philosophy at Princeton University, and before that he was on the faculty at Rockefeller University in Manhattan, among such distinguished and eminent colleagues as Donald Davidson, Harry Frankfurt, and Margaret Wilson.

Kripke's career as a philosopher began in his teens. In 1959 he made his first published professional contribution to philosophy, a paper that formalized an important metatheoretical result in the area of modal logic[4] — the logic underlying the concepts of "necessity" and "possibility." By his mid-twenties he had written a number of foundational papers concerning the semantics of modal logic, and his work is at the fundamentals of the area to this day.[5] By age 30 (in 1970) Kripke had made a contribution to the philosophy of language and mind that definitively changed the way a complex set of historically interrelated issues were considered from that moment on. Shortly thereafter, at age 33, Kripke gave the John Locke lectures at Oxford, a prestigious invitation bestowed on philosophers with the highest intellectual credentials. By the age of 40, Kripke had some claim to having put analytic philosophy, in the tradition of Frege, Russell and Wittgenstein, back on the map. And there was more to come.

His ideas, his youth at the time of their development, his intellectual intensity, the scope and influence of his work: all of these contribute to an inordinate fascination with Kripke the man. Perhaps more than any other philosopher of the 20th century (the exception is Wittgenstein[6], if anyone), Kripke the man and Kripke the philosopher seem inseparable. He has riveted the profession for years, as evidenced by any number of what are smilingly called 'Kripke anecdotes,' passed on from link to link. But there is no denying that it is Kripke's work that is the most powerful and remarkable influence on the substance of late 20th century philosophy. No current discussion of description theories of meaning, externalist theories of meaning, contingent identity, the mind-body problem, possible worlds, Wittgenstein's rule-following considerations, the private language argument, or semantic paradoxes, to name just a few issues, can fail to refer to the work of Saul Kripke.

In what follows, I will discuss three of Kripke's most significant contributions to philosophy. In Chapter 1 I examine the basis and significance of Kripke's work on the semantics of modal logic. In Chapter 2, I explain and comment on the issues that arise in the series of lectures known as *Naming and Necessity* (Kripke 1980). In Chapter 3, I will critically examine Kripke's views on Wittgenstein, published in *Wittgenstein: On Rules and Private Language* (Kripke 1982). Kripke has published other work, and may yet publish still more — but these books and papers alone could more than establish him as the greatest living philosopher; as we will see.[7]

First-order Logic and the Development of Modal Logic

Logical form and grammatical form

Kripke's work in modal logic was groundbreaking, but it is not particularly accessible to a non-specialist reader (someone with little or no background in logic or mathematics). The work takes the form of a technical exposition of formal results, so in order to understand its impact, we must turn our attention first to the concerns of non-modal symbolic logic, in order to see how modal logic developed from those beginnings. This will serve to set Kripke's contributions in context.

What is known generally as symbolic logic is concerned with the logical structure of certain kinds of sentences, and the inferences that can be traced from that structure. The logical skeleton of a sentence, once revealed, enables us to track, entirely mechanically, what can be correctly inferred from it (or any sentence that exemplifies the relevant structure). The rules that enable us to do this are generally applicable, symbolically specified, and, because they operate entirely mechanically, they have predictable results. The benefit of this is the extension of knowledge from what is assumed or known to be true to what can be discovered to follow (to also be true) from the starting points.

Aristotle was the first to specify a number of forms and rules for sentences of simple grammatical subject/predicate form. In the late 19th and early 20th century, however, Frege and Russell, as well as Peirce,[8] all independently, came to realize that Aristotle's formalization was too narrow, depending as it did on grammatical sentential subject/predicate form. The discoverers of modern logic realized that there was more to logical form than grammar, and developed an extension of Aristotelian logic, one that represents the beginning of contemporary philosophical logic.

For example:

All cats are mammals

All mammals fly

So, all cats fly

is an example of the valid inference that cats fly from the two given premises. Note that a chain of inference can be valid even if it contains false premises; the point is that a valid inference is a question of form and not content. It is a further question whether the given premises are actually true.

Aristotle had tabulated the forms of valid inference, in detail, starting with the logical form of four kinds of sentences. The logical form of these was based on membership relations between two groups of things: the things referred to by the grammatical subject of the sentences and those referred to by the grammatical predicate. What are known as Aristotle's categorical propositions take the following four forms:

All S is P

No S is P

Some S is P

Some S is not P.

Each of these four forms, in turn, could be combined with the others in such a way as to generate a number of valid chains of inference. The above example, for instance, is valid according to the form: All A is B, All B is C, so All A is C. But what of:

Michael is taller than Gary

Gary is taller than Tom

So, Michael is taller than Tom.

Aristotle had determined no method for determining the validity of argument forms where the chain of inference consists of, for instance, a deduction from a relation borne between two or more individual particulars; in the above argument, the relation *taller than* drives the deduction. What the discoverers of symbolic logic came to see was that there were more valid argument forms to be revealed in the sub-structure of a sentence than Aristotle had realized.

It turns out that the logical form of a sentence is better specified, for logical purposes, in terms of the structure of function/argument, familiar in mathematics. What this means is that what counts as a logical subject will not, in many cases, conform to grammar. Grammatically, "Michael is taller than Gary" has "Michael" as a subject. But this is too crude, logically and formally speaking, to support the above inference (intuitively, a clearly legitimate one). It is, logically speaking, odd to claim that the structure of the above inference turns on the subject 'Michael' possessing the property 'taller than Gary'; that is, as Aristotle would have to claim, that the subject class of "All Michaels" belongs to the predicate class of "taller than Garys." The property *taller than* is not a singular property, like the property of being red — it is a relation between more than one thing.

The structure of function/argument is more subtle, and is able to account for, among others, the type of inference illustrated in the above example. Loosely speaking, for our purposes, this is a structure that is primarily logically expressed by words that refer to the properties or characteristics that are possessed by individuals. Some of those properties can be singularly instantiated or possessed by an individual ("Tom is human"), but some are, logically speaking, relations between

4

particular individuals ("Michael is taller than Tom").

Gottlob Frege (1848-1925), a German mathematician, is credited with having realized that far more valid argument forms can be tabulated by assessing the logical form of a sentence with respect to the terms that refer to properties, their instantiations, and how many those instantiations number (what is known as quantification). Aristotle, and even Leibniz,[9] had been for various reasons convinced that every sentence was or could be made to conform to subject/predicate structure. But, as we saw above, there are counterexamples to this conviction, involving predicate terms that appear, more accurately, to be analyzed as relations rather than singular properties. In addition to the pressure on the Aristotelian notion of logical form coming from relational properties, however, there is also pressure that comes from the discovery of quantification. A sentence like

> Everyone thinks everyone is an only child[10]

can show that there is something amiss in the Aristotelian analysis of formal structure. Is 'everyone' a subject term like 'Aristotle'? Does it, that is, refer to an individual particular? How does the inference

> Everyone thinks everyone is an only child
>
> Someone is an only child
>
> Therefore, everyone thinks someone is an only child

proceed, according to the Aristotelian notion of logical form? Given examples like this, it is generally believed that there are intuitive chains of inference that Aristotle's system had no way of explaining or providing a calculus for.

These are the basics of first-order symbolic logic.[11] The relevance to the development of modal logic lies in the method for interpreting the symbolic forms of first-order logic, and calculating their valid consequences.

The Truth-Functional Connectives

Simple subject/predicate sentences can be made more complex by linking them to others. What are known as the truth-functional connectives of basic propositional logic achieve this purpose. One of the key ways to formulate logical complexity is by way of the principle that the whole sentence is composed of parts, and that the truth-value of the whole is a function of the truth-value of the parts. For instance:

Tom is at the Garden

Gary is in Soho

So, Tom is at the Garden and Gary is in Soho.

The conclusion is a conjunction of the two premises, and is true only if both of the premises are (this is the condition that defines a conjunction, which in English is expressed by the word 'and'). It turns out that there are five truth-functional connectives which provide the logical definition of the expressions 'and,' 'or,' 'not,' 'if...then,' and 'if and only if' (English has more logical form than it may seem). As we saw above, a conjunction is true if and only if ("iff") both conjuncts are true. A disjunction ("or") is true iff at least one disjunct is true. A negation ("not") is true iff the proposition it applies to is false, and false iff the proposition is true. A biconditional ("if and only if") is true iff both sides of the biconditional have the same truth value.

The specification of 'if...then', however, logically referred to as the conditional, has proven to be controversial. The dissatisfaction with the logical specification of the conditional, meant to capture our intuitions about what we want to convey using the expression 'if...then,' was the impetus for the development of modal logic, so we turn our attention to the conditional below.

The Paradoxes of Material Implication

How do we specify the truth of a conditional sentence: what are its truth conditions? The answer given by Frege, and, most notably, by Whitehead and Russell in their groundbreaking *Principia Mathemetica* (Whitehead and Russell, 1910-13), was that a conditional sentence has the logical form of a truth-function, like conjunction, disjunction, etc., above. This means that the truth of a conditional sentence is calculated as a function of the truth of its parts (the antecedent and the consequent). The truth-functional interpretation has it that a conditional sentence is only false when the antecedent is true and the consequent is false, and true in all other cases.

But this interpretation does lead to some unintuitive results. Consider the sentences: 'If the sun orbited the earth, the sun's rays would be stronger than they are now' or 'If there were morphine in tobacco, cigarettes would be more enjoyable.' In cases where we wish to express a connection between the antecedent and the consequent, such that the truth of the consequent is taken as linked to the truth of the antecedent, the question arises how the whole conditional can be true merely if the antecedent is false, or the consequent true. The truth-conditional interpretation of the conditional appears to make any connection between antecedent and consequent irrelevant to the truth of the conditional. But this does not completely accord with our understanding and grasp of conditional sentences; and a logical or formal definition is meant to be a formal definition of what we want to express when we use 'if...then,' one that captures what we take ourselves to mean and understand by that expression.

There is a further difficulty that arises from the standard interpretation of the conditional. It is accepted practice to express arguments themselves as conditionals; a chain of inference is, in effect, a set of premises, which act as the antecedent, and the conclusion is the consequent. Hence, the very notion of validity itself depends on a perspicuous interpretation of the conditional. But the standard interpretation of the conditional has the result that any conditional is true that has either a false antecedent or a true consequent. No other condition is relevant to the truth of the whole conditional proposition, once one of these two obtains. Given this, it might also seem that an argument, composed as it is with premises (antecedents) and a conclusion (a consequent) will be valid, so long as its premises are false, or its conclusion is true.

These remarks introduce the paradoxes of material implication, as they are known. From the truth-functional interpretation of the conditional follow not only the counterintuitive results above, but also these formulae (both appear as theorems in *Principia Mathematica*, in fact)[12]:

$$p \supset (q \supset p)$$

This formula claims that any conditional will be true so long as its consequent is true ('p' and 'q' are variables that stand in for any sentence). This next formula also follows from the truth-functional interpretation of the conditional:

$$\sim p \supset (p \supset q)$$

This says that any conditional will follow from a false antecedent (since if $\sim p$ is true, then p is false.) But this shows that any sentence will imply p, if p is true; or p will imply any sentence, so long as $\sim p$ is true (i.e., p is false). And these results seem to be, if not strictly paradoxical, certainly far more problematic for the truth-functional definition of the conditional given by Frege, and Whitehead and Russell.

Strict Implication

C.I.Lewis,[13] a philosopher at Harvard in the early part of the century, is credited with developing the first formal treatments of what is known as modal logic,[14] stemming from his conviction that there was a need for another analysis of the logical form of the conditional. Lewis was concerned to capture the intuition that some conditionals state a connection between the truth of the antecedent and the truth of the consequent, and attempted to give an analysis of the conditional that captured this intuition. To do so, Lewis introduced to philosophical logic, and ultimately, to metaphysics, a relation he called "strict implication," often symbolized by what is known as a "fishhook" ($\prec$). Strict implication was meant to express the relation between the antecedent and the consequent of a conditional such that a valid inference that takes this form cannot be such that P is true and Q false. The strict implication relation is meant to block the possibility that both P and $\sim Q$ could be true at the same time, for remember that if $\sim Q$ is true, then Q is false, and if Q is false, any conditional with Q as its antecedent will be true. And as we have seen, the standard definition of the material conditional was so weak (this weak, in particular) that it led to the so-called paradoxes of material implication, as above.

So, Lewis argued, for a conditional understood as a strict implication to be true its definition will take the form: it is not possible that both P be true and Q false. And the way that Lewis formulated his discovery, in terms of the impossibility of a certain combination of truth-values, gave rise to the development of modal logic, the logic of statements that refer to necessity (the way things must be), and possibility (the ways things might be).

Necessity and Possibility

Modal logic provides logical definitions and formal principles for inferences involving the concepts of necessity and possibility, but also, and perhaps more important, provides an interpretation for our claims of necessity and possibility. After all, when we say "I might have gone to law school," or "I have to be alive in order to be writing this now," it isn't immediately clear what exactly we are talking about. What does "it's possible" really mean? When we say "p has to be so" what do we mean? What are we referring to? What objects are being talked about? Granted we sometimes speak in hyperbole about what is not possible and what must be so, particularly when in an emotional state, but we all understand it. So what are necessity and possibility meant to apply to? As we will see below, the question is not an easy

8

one; and it is part of the significance of Kripke's contribution to modal logic that he provided an answer to this question.

The De Re/De Dicto Distinction, Deontic, Temporal, and Doxastic Logic

To see the difficulty, we can briefly allude to a distinction that frequently arises in talk of modality, in answer to this question: the so-called *de re/de dicto* distinction. *De re* is the Latin for 'of the thing' and *de dicto* is the Latin for 'of the thing said (or proposition)'. This issue concerns whether necessity or possibility applies to propositions (as some kind of linguistic device) or to individuals and the properties they possess. For instance:

It is necessarily true that nine is odd

claims that 'nine is odd' is a proposition that is necessarily true. Here, necessity is conceived as an operator on sentences (or propositions), and applies to their truth (or falsity); the notion of necessity conceived in this way is what is known as *de dicto* necessity. The alternative conception of necessity, *de re* necessity, is one where the notion of necessity applies to the possession of a property by an individual. Take for instance:

Cats are necessarily mammals

Here the claim is that cats possess a property necessarily — that of being mammals. The necessity claim is understood as a metaphysical one, and not a linguistic one: in this case, it takes the form of claiming that if x is a cat, then x has to be a mammal.

The *de re/de dicto* distinction has inspired controversy, both in itself as well as in relation to modal logic, and there continues to be an unresolved dispute on the question of the proper object of modal discourse. There are further issues, as well, that arise with respect to the objects of modal discourse. Some logicians have been persuaded that the terrain of modal discourse more widely includes moral, temporal and mental concepts. The attempt to formalize these concepts has led to the development of logics in the modal family that are concerned with the logical form of expressions like "It is obligatory (forbidden/permitted) that p" (deontic logic); "It will be/will always be/has always been the case that p" (temporal logic); and "X believes that p" (doxastic logic). However, it is the logic of possibility and necessity—modal logic more narrowly circumscribed — that is our focus here, and we begin our examination of it next.

Modal Logic: Introduction

A logical system, in brief, is constituted by two things; a set of symbols and the rules for combining them; and an interpretation of those symbols. Lewis (1918; 1932) used an axiomatic method based on that of Whitehead and Russell's in *Principia Mathematica* to construct a number of symbolic systems (and the rules for combining formulae in them) that took his notion of strict implication, and not the truth-functional notion of implication, as key. In doing so, Lewis introduced symbolic operators for "possibility," "necessity," and strict implication.[15] The basic and foundational concepts of modal logic — necessity (what must be), impossibility (what cannot be), contingency (what might be), and possibility (what could be) — are, notably, interdefinable, and there is a particular concordance between "possibility" and "necessity." To say that a proposition p is necessarily true, for instance, can be expressed this way: it is not possible that p is false, or:

$$\Box p = \sim\Diamond\sim p$$

Conversely, to say that a proposition p is possibly true is to say that it is not necessary that p is false:

$$\Diamond p = \sim\Box\sim p$$

'$\Box$' and '$\Diamond$' are what are known as monadic operators in the systems of modal logic developed by Lewis. They apply to propositions the way the negation sign ($\sim$) does in non-modal propositional logic; that is, a monadic operator modifies or applies to one proposition. The syntactic rules that specify what is called the "well-formedness" of a negation are such that if P is well formed, then so is $\sim P$. So, for instance, we cannot say $P \sim Q$; this is not a "well-formed formula"— a formula constructed according to the grammatical rules of the system. The rules are what specify which symbolic strings or sequences can legitimately carry meaning in the system (like the rules of English grammar for spelling). Now, since '$\Box$' is a monadic operator like ' $\sim$ ', in modal logic $P \Box Q$ is no more well-formed than is $P \sim Q$.

In contrast to a monadic operator, a dyadic (or triadic, etc.) operator modifies or applies to more than one proposition. Strict implication (like conjunction ['&'] or disjunction ['v']) is a dyadic operator, one that joins two propositions. So, to say that $P \prec Q$ is to say that (as Lewis defined it) it is not possible for P to be true and Q to be false at the same time; or, if P is true, then Q can't be false.

Lewis developed a series of systems on this interpretation of implication. His early book *A Survey of Symbolic Logic* (Lewis 1918) features the system which has come to be known as S3 (that is, *system 3*), which is in part characterized by taking logical impossibility as the primitive modal operator. With the publication of *Symbolic Logic* in 1932, however, Lewis, with his collaborator C.H. Langford, set out, for the first time, detailed axiomatic systems of strict implication, with possibility, instead, as the primitive modal operator. The editor's introduction states (1959, 2nd edition: preface):

> ...Professor Lewis's *A Survey of Symbolic Logic* in 1918 traced the history of the most important developments of symbolic logic from Leibniz to the twentieth century and discussed the relation of a "system of strict implication" to systems of material implication and to the classic algebra of logic. But there has been no authoritative treatment of the field of symbolic logic in the light of developments of the last fifteen years....This present volume is just such a treatment.

The systems developed in the most detail in Lewis and Langford (1932) are known as S1 and S2, and the relations between them and the systems S3, S4 and S5 are given in an appendix written by Lewis himself (1932: 500):

> From the preceding discussion it becomes evident that there is a group of systems of the general type of Strict Implication and each distinguishable from Material Implication. We shall arrange these in the order of increasing comprehensiveness and decreasing 'strictness' of the implication relation.

What this means, in effect, is that each system successively contains the theorems of the others, as we will see in more formal detail below.

Now a logical system consists primarily of symbols and rules for their manipulation, as well as an interpretation of the symbolic strings. But, in fact, one of the most powerful properties of logical systems is that important logical relations can be specified merely syntactically. This means that (for instance) merely by following a specified set of grammatical rules, one symbolic string can be replaced by another, theorems can be proved; deductions can be effected; all quite independent of the meaning assigned to the symbolic strings.

What Lewis developed was the symbolic, structural properties of a series of systems of modal logic: their syntax. And while it is true (both for non-modal propositional logic and modal logic) that many important logical relations can be specified purely syntactically, there

11

are others that cannot. Most important of these is validity. A logical system is one that is meant to specify as precisely as possible the notion of correct inference (good reasoning), based on the intuitive notion that an inference is valid iff it is not possible for the premises to be true and the conclusion false. But with no semantic interpretation for a series of symbolic strings, it is not possible to give an account of what makes an inference valid. No substantive criterion of a correct inference is possible if we cannot specify the conditions under which symbolic strings are true or false. We will discuss this in further detail below.

Of the modal systems that there are, each has its own axioms, and theorems; no system is equivalent to the others. Some systems are stronger than others, in that the consequences or theorems of one system are a subset of the theorems of another. What makes one system stronger or weaker than another turns on the issue of the logical relations that can or cannot be captured with the resources available to that system. In fact, what the variety of modal systems does is highlight the lack of a formal and unifying definition for (among other things) validity; we must ask, for each system, what the criterion of validity will be. This of course raises the issue of which system is the correct system: that is, which system correctly captures inferences that involve claims about necessity and possibility.

The problem stems in part from the fact that modal operators are not defined truth functionally, as we saw above in the case of non-modal propositional logic. The connectives are defined truth-functionally; any sentence subject to modification by a connective is either true or false, and the truth-value of the whole resulting proposition will be a function of the truth-value of its parts, according to the rules that specify the truth-value of the connective in question. There are, moreover, further logical properties of propositions that can be determined by a truth-functional evaluation of the truth-value assignments to their parts. For example, a logical truth is defined as a sentence that is true under every truth-value assignment ('p or $\sim p$', to take one example). A sentence of the form 'p or $\sim p$' is true whether p is true or whether p is false, given the definition of a disjunctive sentence ('or') that a disjunction is true iff at least one of the disjuncts is true.

But the truth-conditions of $\Box p$, or $\Diamond p$, are not a simple function from the truth-value of p. Notice that if p is true, then $\Diamond p$ is true; since if p is true, then the logical possibility of p is assured. But $\Diamond p$ is also true when $\sim p$ is true. Just because p is false does not rule out that it is possible that p could be true; and if we can't rule out that p couldn't be true, then it is possible that p is true. The cat is not in the drawer, for instance, but he *could* have been. So if p could be true (even though

12

~p), then ◊p is true. So we do not have a definitive result calculable from a truth-value assignment to p for ◊p.

The situation is similar for □p. If p is false, then we know that it cannot be necessary that p; for p to be necessary is for p to never fail to be true. However, if p is true, it won't follow that □p. P could be merely contingently true, and not necessarily true — sometimes true, not always true (the cat is in the drawer, but he didn't *have* to be.). So, again, we do not have a definitive result for □p given a truth-value assigned to p.

The situation becomes even more pressing when we realize that the modal operators can be iterated, or repeated in strings (just like negation). If we do not have a clear criterion of the truth-value of □p or ◊p what can we make of ◊□p, □◊p, □□p, or ◊◊p? And what of strings of modal operators greater than two?

Now, as we will see below, there are purely syntactic solutions available for a number of issues involving inferential relations between modal formulae containing operators singly or in strings. But it wasn't until Saul Kripke (among others) developed his ideas on the semantics of modal logic that there was a clear way of interpreting and understanding modal propositions, and of formally specifying validity and other semantic properties of the systems. In order to put Kripke's semantics for modal logic in context, we begin with some of the formal differences between the systems known as T, S4, S5, and B,[16] below.

The Modal Systems T, S4, S5, and B: Formal Properties and Distinctions

One useful way to introduce and discuss these systems is by way of a set of criteria that any system should fulfill to be interpreted as a modal system, as follows:[17]

1. Since possibility and necessity are intuitively interdefinable, a system should specify which operator will be taken as primitive.

2. Strict implication is the relation between p and q when and only when it is impossible for p to be true without q also being true. Two propositions that strictly imply each other are strictly equivalent.

3. P prefixed by a modal operator cannot be equivalent to p or any truth-function involving p.

4. The following axioms should be part of the system: the so-called axiom of necessity, which claims that whatever is necessarily true is true; and the so-called axiom of possibility; which claims that whatever is true is possible.

5. Any proposition that has the form of a valid formula is necessarily true.

6. Whatever follows from a necessary truth is itself necessarily true.

Now, given the number of modal systems there are, we need a rough sketch of the connections between systems and their development, with emphasis, in particular, on those systems to which the conditions for modal system candidacy cited above apply.[18] Feys (1937) developed the system T (he called it 't'). Sobociński (1953) showed that T (what he called Feys' system 't') is equivalent to von Wright's (1951) system M, and the names "T" and "M" are sometimes used interchangeably. As we noted above, Lewis (Lewis and Langford 1932) developed the systems S1 and S2; S3, S4 and S5 are developed in Appendix II (1932) and Appendix III ((added in 1959 in the second edition): 492-514). Becker (1930) is credited with the so-called "reduction axioms" which form one basis for distinction between T and S4 and S5, as formalized in Hughes and Cresswell (1968).[19] The system B is historically named after the mathematician Brouwer; the axiom that distinguishes the system B from the others is derived from Becker (1930).[20]

T is the weakest system that conforms to the conditions above. It is the weakest system in that the theses of T are also theses of other systems (other sytems contain T), which themselves contain theses that are not theses of T. We can begin by comparing T to S4 and then to S5. The following definitions simplify the task:[21]

1. A modality is an unbroken sequence of zero or more monadic operators ($\sim$, $\Box$, $\Diamond$).

2. A modality is iterated iff it contains two or more modal operators.

3. Two modalities are equivalent in a given system if the result of replacing one by the other in any formula is always equivalent in that system to the original formula.

4. Reduction laws express the reducibility of certain modalities to others in systems of which they are theses.

Now, what distinguishes T from S4 and S5 is that S4 and S5 contain what are known as reduction laws. These laws in effect permit the reduction of strings of iterated modal operators. Reduction laws are important because they govern the number of types of modalities in a system; that is, they regulate the number of combination sequences of the operators '~', '□', and '◊' that may occur. In addition, they capture and simplify, formally, intuitive inferences that make use of iterated modalities.

We can start with some important modal aspects of T.[22] T takes □ as primitive, and defines ◊ as:

$$\sim\square\sim p.$$

In T, strict implication is defined as $\square\ (p \supset q)$, and for p to be equivalent to q means both that p strictly implies q and q strictly implies p. Further, there are two important axioms (conditions 4 and 6, p. 14, above) that play a role in T:

The Axiom of Necessity: $\square p \supset p$

The Distribution Axiom: $\square\ (p \supset q\ ) \supset (\square\, p \supset \square\, q)$.

T also contains what is known as the Rule of Necessitation, which claims that if any modal formula is a thesis, then it is not just true but necessarily true (condition 5, p. 14, above).

Now, there are other important aspects of T as a system. Since it has no reduction laws among its theses, it contains infinitely many distinct modalities.[23] Furthermore, no iterated modalities play a role in any of its theses. The issue of iterated modalities is important both from the perspective of the syntactical, formal properties of systems, and also from the perspective of the interpretation or semantics of a given system. Given a modal formula like:

$$\square p \supset \square\square p$$

we might wonder: is it valid? Intuitively, the claim is that if p is necessarily true, then it follows that it is necessarily true that p is necessarily true. But on the face of it, the truth (or falsity) of the formula (in fact, the inference) may be hard to assess; for under what conditions is a proposition necessarily necessarily true? Are we even sure we know what this means?

Now, if perplexity concerning the interpretation of modal formulae containing iterated modal operators starts with a relatively simple example such as that above, then what are we to make of the following modal formula:

15

$$\sim ((\ \Box\Diamond\Box\Diamond\Box\Box\Diamond\Diamond p) \ \& \ \sim(\Box\Diamond\Diamond p))$$

This is the negation of a conjunction, one of whose conjuncts is itself a negation. The first conjunct reads something like this:

> It is necessarily possibly necessarily possibly necessarily necessarily possibly possible that p

The other conjunct, a negation, reads

> It is not the case that (it is necessarily possibly possible that p)

It is similarly not obvious what this formula means, let alone whether it is valid. But it is perplexities like these that highlight the issue of how to manage modal formulae with iterated operators. The distinction between T and S4, and between T and S5[24] is a way of providing an answer, since we can't provide an answer with the resources available in T. We need the reduction laws to better manage formulae that contain iterated operators, which S4 and S5 contain.

Reduction laws are equivalences that permit us to replace a sequence of modal operators by another, shorter, sequence. The following are four important equivalences that could act as reduction laws[25]:

> 1. $\Diamond p \equiv \Box\Diamond p$
> (if possibly p, then p must be possible)
> 2. $\Box p \equiv \Diamond\Box p$
> (if necessarily p, then it is possible that p is necessarily true)
> 3. $\Diamond p \equiv \Diamond\Diamond p$
> (if possibly p, then it is possible that p is possible)
> 4. $\Box p \equiv \Box\Box p$
> (if necessarily p, then it is a necessary truth that p is a necessary truth)

S4 is a system that is constructed by adding ($\Box p \supset \Box\Box p$) to T, which is one half of the equivalence in #4, above. S5 is a system constructed by adding ($\Diamond p \supset \Box\Diamond p$), half of the equivalence in #1, above, to T. This latter highlights one metaphysical issue that lurks behind the results of these formal systems: namely, the issue as to whether modal properties are possessed *necessarily*. The theorems that define S4 and S5 give an affirmative answer to this issue, but in a weaker and stronger form, respectively. That is, it does not follow from the fact that all necessary propositions are necessarily necessary (provable in S4) that all *possible* propositions are necessarily possible (provable in S5).[26]

T is weaker than S4 and S5, and its theorems are contained in both; and S4 is weaker than S5. S4 contains an interesting result with respect to the kinds of formulae that it contains: it turns out that there are at most 14 different modalities in S4. Given the S4 reduction laws, every modality will take one of the following seven forms or its negation:

The zero case: no monadic operators

1. $\square$
2. $\Diamond$
3. $\square\Diamond$
4. $\Diamond\square$
5. $\square\Diamond\square$
6. $\Diamond\square\Diamond$

S5 is even more compact. All four equivalences, above, are theorems of S5, and result in a rule that states that in any sequence of monadic modal operators, all but the last one may be deleted.[27] This has the result that S5 has at most *six* different modalities, which will take one of these three forms or its negation:

1. the zero case

2. $\square$

3. $\Diamond$

This is a powerful result, given the exigencies of interpreting formulae containing strings of modal operators. To see this, we can apply it to our example above (p. 16):

$$\sim ((\ \square\Diamond\square\Diamond\square\square\Diamond\Diamond p)\ \&\ \sim(\square\Diamond\Diamond p))$$

The result is this:

$$\sim ((\Diamond p)\ \&\ \sim\Diamond p)$$

which turns out to be the modal version of the simple and straightforward law of logic that claims that a proposition *and* its negation cannot both be true. This example provides a graphic way of appreciating the strength of certain formal operations applicable to the symbolic strings that comprise the modal systems we are considering here.

We conclude this brief review of the syntactic relations between these modal systems by commenting on the system known as B. What is interesting, formally speaking, is that B is formed either by adding the theorem:

$$p \supset \Box \Diamond p$$

or the theorem:

$$\Diamond \Box p \supset p$$

to the system T.[28] If either theorem were added to S4, the result would be S5. Adding these theorems to T, instead, results in B, a system that is weaker than S5, but neither contains nor is contained by S4.

The formalization of modal axioms, principles, and laws (both sentential and quantificational) was no small achievement, but as we earlier remarked, Lewis (and others) were able to specify only a syntax for the modal systems the developed. Without a semantics, however, or an interpretation of what the formal principles might be about, the situation was something like the case of the non-Italian speaker learning the rules of Italian grammar and only those rules. Imagine if you were asked to learn only the grammar of Italian: the alphabet, the rules for combining letters into words, and words into sentences, spelling, etc…but you were never told what your perfectly produced symbolic strings meant, what they referred to, or what they were about. You could know all those grammatical rules, but you still wouldn't know Italian, if this were the case. This was the situation with respect to modal logic, which changed with the publication of Kripke's papers "A Completeness Theorem in Modal Logic (Kripke 1959)," "Semantical Considerations on Modal Logic" (Kripke 1963a), and "Semantical Analysis of Modal Logic" (Kripke 1963).

Possible Worlds Semantics

We seem to have a strong intuitive sense of alternative ways things could have gone, or ways things could be. We also, interestingly, have a (maybe slightly less) strong intuitive sense at which point such alternatives stop being plausible — for instance, it seems I could still be me and not live on 64th street, but I couldn't be me and be a tree, or an island. The notion of what is or is not possible is at the basis of Kripke's contribution to the semantics of modal logic.[29] What Kripke claimed was that modal discourse is best understood as discourse that refers to possible *worlds*, of which our world, the actual world, is only one of many (Kripke 1959: 3):

> In modal logic…we wish to know not only about the real world but about other conceivable worlds; P may be true in the real world but false in some imaginable one….

It is *true* in the actual world, for instance, that I am a philosopher; but in another possible world, one related to the actual world such that everything is the same except that (say) I chose law school instead of graduate school in philosophy, it is *false* that I am a philosopher. Though in that world it is false that I am a philosopher, it is nevertheless *possible* that I am a philosopher. I *might have been* a philosopher, even though, in that world, I am not. So $\Diamond p$ is true, though p is false.

One way of understanding the significance Kripke's contributions to modal logic is to note that what Kripke did was to make it far more clear what it could mean to say that it is true that *I could have been* (say) a paramedic or an electrician — calculably clear, in fact. Kripke specified a set of entities that could act as the object of modal discourse, but he also specified a set of criteria by which to assess the *truth-value* of modal claims.

This wasn't all. Recall that prior to work in the semantics of modal logic, modal systems were understood as purely formal, and as such, lacked two important elements. First, it was unclear how to understand the formulae; that is, how to give an interpretation of them so that they could be more easily seen to express our talk about necessity and possibility, formally speaking. Second, formal systems did not provide an account of the concepts of validity or of completeness, critical to any formal system, but not specifiable by way of purely formal means. We noted above that validity is one of the most important semantic notions that attach to a formal system of logic. Another is *completeness*: a property of formal systems such that in systems that are complete, every valid well-formed formula of the system is derivable as a thesis in the system. A stronger claim is that the system cannot posses any more theses than it does without becoming *inconsistent*.[30] Consistency is yet another property of systems, such that no consistent system will contain rules or definitions that will enable the derivation of a thesis *and* its negation.

Completeness builds on the concept of validity, in that it concerns the laws and principles that reveal the strength of the system in question. For an inferential system to be reliable, we must be able to show that all and only valid chains of inference are so provable given the resources—the laws, axioms, and principles—of that system. Notoriously, for instance, Kurt Gödel proved that arithmetic was *incomplete*; i.e., that there were arithmetical truths not formally provable.[31] For classical systems of logic, however, completeness is possible (something Gödel himself first proved in 1930).[32] And among Kripke's results for modal logic was showing there was a way of

19

proving completeness for modal logic as well.

We can better understand the significance of Kripke's contribution to the semantics of modal logic by recalling a problem we noted above. As we saw there, the difference in specifying semantic notions for the formulae in a non-modal system and those in a modal system is that modal operators do not behave truth-functionally. What Kripke was able to was provide a way of understanding modal operators that built on a familiar device in non-modal logic: the quantifier. Quantifiers specify, logically speaking, how many individual particulars a property or relation is instantiated by. What Kripke claimed was that the modal operators 'necessarily' and 'possibly' could be understood to behave logically like the quantifiers 'All' and 'Some'—in effect, that they *were* quantifiers, quantifiers over what he called "possible worlds." The allusion to Leibniz's claim that necessary truth is truth in all possible worlds is the source for the name traditionally given to Kripke's results in the semantics of modal logic: possible worlds semantics.

Treating modal operators as quantifiers over possible worlds means that truth, validity, completeness and consistency will not be determined by modal formulae in isolation. At the basis of this idea is a crucial difference between the semantics of modal logic and the semantics of non-modal logic. The latter specifies the truth-conditions of a proposition by assigning a truth-value (either *true* or *false*) to its parts. The truth-value of the whole is a function of the truth-value of *its* parts; *other* propositions, their atomic parts, and the truth-value assignments to those parts are not relevant. For instance, to determine the validity of a non-modal formula of propositional logic, we construct a *truth-table*, which is a kind of truth-value abacus. A truth-table graphically assigns truth-values to the parts of the proposition and then to the whole, constructed from those parts, according to the truth-conditions for the connectives present in the formula. All that is left to do after constructing a truth-table for a formula is to *read off* the results. A valid argument, for instance, is one that contains *no* line on its truth-table that has a "T" in the column under the premises at the same time as an "F" in the column under the conclusion.

But, as we have noted, there are no truth-tables for the modal operators. The truth-value of modal propositions, instead, must be assessed taking a set of *possible worlds* in which they might be true or false into consideration, with the modal operators themselves interpreted as quantifiers over either *all* possible worlds (the reading of '□') or *some* possible world (the reading of '◊'). The fundamental idea is that semantic notions like validity and completeness will be defined

20

and specified in terms of models composed of sets of worlds, along with restrictions on the relation between these worlds. It turns out that the different systems of modal logic can be represented as corresponding to different restrictions on the relation between worlds.

Possible Worlds Semantics: The Accessibility Relation

The specification of the truth-conditions for a modal formula involves what has been called a *frame*. This is a structure stipulated to formally contain:

1. A set **W** of all possible worlds

2. The (dyadic) relation **R** of accessibility (world to world)

According to Kripke, the semantic interpretation of modal formulae turns on a determination of **R,** the so-called accessibility relation. It is the restrictions on the accessibility relation **R** that ground the characteristic theorems of different modal systems. A *model* on a frame will add one more element to the set containing **W** and **R** (as above): what is called a 'valuation function.' This is a function from truth-values to formulae at worlds. We will see, informally, how this works below.

Now, what is **R** (variously referred to as "accessibility," "relative possibility," and "conceivability")? Here we will adopt "accessibility" for convenience, and spell out what is behind this concept. The accessibility relation builds on the intuition that to assess the truth-value of a modal claim requires us to take circumstances (worlds) other than actual ones into consideration. It is further intuitive to claim that some worlds will be *possible* given the facts of the actual world and some are *impossible* given those facts. An example given by David Lewis illustrates the idea (1972: 1):

> ... '*If kangaroos had no tails, they would topple over*' seems to me to mean something like this: in any possible state of affairs in which kangaroos have no tails, and which resembles our actual state of affairs as much as kangaroos having no tails permits it to, the kangaroos topple over.

We know that the truth-conditions of $\Box p$ and $\Diamond p$ (in the actual world) will have to take into consideration facts about other worlds, on Kripke's view. But we can stipulate that the worlds we consider are *accessible from the actual world*, or *possible given the facts of the actual world*, and characterize the accessibility relation in question. To clothe the idea, however, we can say the worlds accessible from the actual world resemble it as much as the counterfactual circumstances permit it. A world of tailless kangaroos, for instance, probably resembles the actual world of kangaroos and their tails enough for us to say that such a world is accessible from the actual world. A world inaccessible from the actual world, instead, will contain circumstances downright impossible relative to the states of affairs in the actual world (a world where (what are called) 'kangaroos' aren't mammals, perhaps).

Now, the interpretations of the modal operators from this perspective are as follows:[33]

> 1. $\Diamond p$ is true at the actual world (call it $\mathbf{w}^*$) if p is true at *some* world in $\mathbf{W}$ that is accessible to $\mathbf{w}^*$.
>
> 2. $\Box p$ is true at the actual world $\mathbf{w}^*$ if p is true at *all* worlds in $\mathbf{W}$ accessible to $\mathbf{w}^*$.

Given these two rules governing the interpretation of modal operators, as well as the truth-functions for the non-modal connectives, we have a way of calculating truth-values of modal formulae, as we will see.

One of Kripke's notable results was to show that the modal systems were more *structurally* related (in spite of their syntactic and semantic distinctness) than had been suspected in previous work in modal logic. The way he did this, in part, was to characterize the accessibility relation between worlds in a given set $\mathbf{W}$ as either *reflexive, transitive,* or *symmetrical.* For each of the modal systems we considered syntactically, above, we can give a semantic interpretation; and, as the systems are syntactically distinct from one another, we expect their semantics to reflect this. What Kripke did was to characterize the kind of accessibility relation between worlds that would hold in each model, in order to give a way of semantically capturing the differences between modal systems.

A set of worlds $\mathbf{W}$ is a domain of discourse; it is a way of delimiting what the claims of the formulae are about, in whatever systems we are interested in. An analogy with non-modal logic can help to clarify this idea. Learning the rules of natural deduction for the truth-functional connectives can be done wholly syntactically: we learn that if '*A* & *B*' is present on one line of a derivation, we can decompose it into two other lines; *A,* and also *B*. We don't have to know what the variable letters mean to be able to employ this rule. But when a semantics or an interpretation of the symbols is given, it is given by first specifying what is called a domain of discourse. We specify or

22

stipulate what it is that the symbols stand for within that domain. In a domain of discourse comprising Major League baseball teams and (a set of) their properties, A, for instance, might stand for the sentence "The Yankees won the World Series" and B might stand for the sentence "The Mets won the World Series." In a domain of discourse comprised of breeds of dogs and (a set of) their properties, however, A might stand for the sentence "The bull terrier is playful." The point is that *we* stipulate the meaning of our symbols.[34]

The very same thing is true in modal logic. The difference is that to interpret symbolic formulae containing modal operators we have to take account of *other* circumstances (worlds) to establish the truth of a modal claim in (say for convenience) the actual world. So we must specify a domain of discourse; a set of worlds **W** against which we will spell out the truth-conditions of various modal formulae.

We can build on this to show that a characteristic formula of the system T is valid:

$$p \supset \Diamond p$$

The accessibility relation **R** is specified as reflexive for T according to Kripke. So we say that (informally) a T-model will include a set of worlds **W**; and **R** is the (dyadic) reflexive relation between members of **W**. What we want to know is whether the above formula is valid, and to show this, we can stipulate **W** as a set of just one world (for simplicity); the actual world (**w***). On the semantic definition of '$\Diamond$,' we know that $\Diamond p$ is true if, in at least one world in W that is accessible to **w*** in W, p is either true or false. Now our formula above claims that p is true on **w***. And, since **R** is reflexive, we also know that p is true in at least one world accessible to the actual world in **W** — the actual world itself. So the formula is valid.

Recall that, as we saw above, adding the following theorem to T generates the system B:

$$p \supset \Box \Diamond p$$

Again, we specify the truth-conditions at a set of worlds **W**, among which is the actual world **w***. We now need to set conditions on the accessibility relation between worlds to enable the above inference to succeed. Since B contains T, we know that the accessibility relation will be reflexive (every world is accessible to itself), and we stipulate that it will also be symmetrical, to support this case. A symmetrical accessibility relation between worlds is such that for any pair of worlds, each will be accessible from the other. In a model containing three worlds, for instance:

$$w^* \leftrightarrow W2$$

are symmetrically accessible one from the other (shown by the arrows), and:

$$W2 \leftrightarrow W3$$

are symmetrically accessible one from the other, but it won't follow, by symmetry alone, that:

$$W3 \leftrightarrow w^*$$

So (unless we introduce other modifications to the accessibility relation), W3 and w^* are not accessible to each other.

Returning to the B axiom, how can we show that the formula holds at w^*? One thing we can try is to show that a contradiction holds. For instance, we can try to prove the hypothesis that $\sim[p \ \& \ \Box\Diamond p]$ is the case; we can try to prove that the negation of our formula holds. This amounts to showing that not both p and $\Box\Diamond p$ can be true in the actual world. If the relationship between worlds in our model supports this hypothesis, we know the formula isn't valid. If it does not, we know that the formula is valid.

We can stipulate that p is true at w^* and W2, and false at W3, since there are no modal operators involved (the truth value of p doesn't depend on how things are in other worlds). Now, since our hypothesis is that not both p and $\Box\Diamond p$ can be true at the actual world, and we are stipulating to the truth of p, it should follow (if our hypothesis is correct), that $\sim[\Box\Diamond p]$ will hold at w^*.

But in fact, it doesn't. As we know, the truth-conditions of $\Box p$ are such that $\Box p$ is true if p is true in every world accessible from w^* in a model $\mathbf{W}$. As p is true in w^* and W2, we can claim that $\Box p$ is true as well (by reflexivity and symmetry). W3 is accessible from W2, by symmetry, but not from w^*, so we can disregard the fact that p is false at W3 in calculating the truth-conditions of $\Box p$ here.

So what about $\Box\Diamond p$? For this to be true, $\Diamond p$ must be true in all worlds accessible from w^*. We know that p is true at w^*, so we also know that $\Diamond p$ is true both at w^* (by reflexivity) and at W2 (by symmetry) — any formula of the form $\Diamond p$ is true if there is at least one world where p is true accessible from w^* in $\mathbf{W}$. It is but a short step to showing that $\Box\Diamond p$ is true, given what we have established here. $\Box\Diamond p$ is true if $\Diamond p$ is true at every world accessible from w^* in $\mathbf{W}$; and we have established that this is so: it is true in w^* and W2, the two worlds accessible by reflexivity and symmetry to w^*. And if $\Box\Diamond p$ is true, then

~ [$\Box \Diamond p$] isn't true. The formula above is valid.

We can examine the semantics for S4 the same way. What is known as the S4 axiom is:

$$\Box p \supset \Box \Box p$$

For S4, the accessibility relation is specified as reflexive and transitive. That is, consider a set of worlds **W** containing the actual world **w***, W2, and W3. Transitivity means that if W2 is accessible from **w***, and W3 is accessible from W2, then W3 is accessible from **w***. Now, if we stipulate that p is true in all three worlds, then we can claim that $\Box p$ is also true. P is true in all worlds accessible from **w***; it is true in **w*** (by reflexivity); true in W2, and true in W3, and these worlds are accessible from **w***, given the constraints to our model.

Now to show that the S4 axiom is valid, we can try the hypothesis that ~[$\Box \Box p$] holds in the actual world — we can try to show that there is a world accessible from **w*** where a contradiction to $\Box \Box p$ is true. But, in fact, we will not succeed. We have already shown that $\Box p$ is true. So $\Box \Box p$ is true if, at all worlds accessible from **w***, $\Box p$ is true. We showed this above: if $\Box p$ is true at **w***, then it is true at W2 and at W3 by transitivity, and at each of those worlds by reflexivity. There is no world accessible from **w*** where it is not the case that $\Box \Box p$ holds; so the S4 axiom is valid.

Finally, since S5 contains S4, B, and T, the model for S5 will define the accessibility relation between worlds as reflexive, transitive and symmetrical — incorporating all of the elements that are model-constituents for each of the other modal systems. What is known as the S5 axiom is:

$$\Diamond p \supset \Box \Diamond p$$

To show this is valid, we stipulate a set of worlds **W**, one of which we call the actual world **w***. We further stipulate p as true in all our worlds (for simplicity). If p is true in **w***, then $\Diamond p$ is also true (since p is true in at least one world in **W** accessible to **w***). Now, is $\Box \Diamond p$ also true? We know that $\Diamond p$ is true, in fact, in all worlds accessible to **w***, given that the accessibility relation is specified as reflexive, transitive, and symmetrical. So $\Box \Diamond p$ is true, and the axiom is valid.

This brief examination of the application of possible worlds semantics to some of the systems of modal logic should be enough to indicate the power and adaptability of this way of interpreting modal claims. Possible worlds semantics was an important step forward in the formalization of modal logic. Not only were the concepts of necessity and possibility given substance, but claims that make use of them could be better formalized and systematized. Kripke's accessibility restrictions make the notion of a possible world itself more specific. Possible worlds semantics allows us to prove that the formulae derivable in one of a number of different systems are valid, but, at the same time, keeps the basics of the different systems distinct (or, less charitably, highlights their weaknesses). Modal talk is now not just clarified, but, more importantly, the theorems of the different modal systems are now unified and seen to be structurally related. What appeared as a panoply of different and independent systems are now conceived of as nested and harmonious building blocks in a bigger picture. What Kripke was ultimately able to do through the development of possible worlds semantics was to enable a practically exponential progress of modal logic—both on its more narrow definition and its more general definition. Possible worlds semantics has been applied to deontic, temporal and epistemic logic, for instance, and new areas continue to be explored.

Possible Worlds, Meaning, and Reference

Kripke published his work in modal logic between 1959 and 1963, but he appears to have been busy formulating other ideas at roughly the same time[35] — ideas we will examine in Chapters 2 and 3 below. The notion of possible worlds, for example, may have become far more greatly accessible to philosophers (and even to the public), as a result of the lectures Kripke gave at Princeton in 1970, which have gone down in history under the title *Naming and Necessity*.

In *Naming and Necessity*, the device of possible worlds was employed to make a number of surprising claims about meaning, reference, naming, necessity, truth, and identity, to name a few of the topics treated. The lectures had an extraordinary impact on philosophy. *Naming and Necessity* changed the way the philosophy of language was done, and, unlike most work in philosophy, changed it immediately. Thirty years later the lectures are an indispensable reference for work done on a wide variety topics in the philosophy of language, philosophy of mind, and metaphysics. The examples Kripke used — not to mention the vocabulary he coined — have become absorbed so completely into the literature that they seem like monuments to the concepts that characterize late 20th century analytic philosophy. We turn to *Naming and Necessity* next.

ENDNOTES

[1] Branch (1977).

[2] Branch (1977).

[3] Kripke, in conversation.

[4] Kripke (1959).

[5] Kripke (1963).

[6] See Chapter 3, below.

[7] I must sacrifice extensive commentary on, specifically, Kripke's work on belief, on reference, and his theory of truth. For comment on Kripke's paper "A Puzzle About Belief," see Chapter 2, below.

Kripke's theory of truth (Kripke, 1975) is too formal to allow for detailed consideration here. We can say briefly, however, that Kripke's theory tackles the problem of the liar paradox, a flaw that arises in theories of truth. The paradox arises when it appears that a sentence can *self*-refer. In the classic example, a Cretan who says "All Cretans are liars" is making a claim about truth-telling, but also, it turns out, making a claim *about* the claim. If it's true that all Cretans are liars, then they *don't tell the truth* — about being liars. If they aren't telling the truth about *being liars*, then they're telling the truth. But if they're telling the truth, they're lying. And so on. Kripke considers the problem from the perspective of natural languages (not just logical languages, as in prior work on this issue), and sheds light on the empirical sources of the paradox. His solution (or the outline of one) is one that suggests that in some circumstances, some sentences may not have truth-values at all, which is tantamount to abandoning a classical logical principle that every sentence must be either true or false.

[8] Frege (1879); Russell (1910-13); Peirce (1930-58).

[9] Russell (1918).

[10] Saul Kripke made this observation to me in conversation (but in another context). It appealed to me, so I import it here as an example of multiple quantification.

[11] 'First-order' because the sentences in question are about *individuals* and properties. 'Second-order' logic is concerned with the *properties of properties.*

[12] Hughes and Cresswell (1968:18).

[13] Lewis (1918;1932; (1959 2nd edition)).

[14] At least for sentential or subject/predicate sentences. Modal axioms for quantified sentences came later (Marcus, 1993). Note that in what follows I must exclude discussion of the issue of modality and quantification, as it leads us too far astray from Kripke's specific contributions to modal logic, philosophy of language, and the like.

[15] See Hughes and Cresswell (1968:347-48) for a history of the use of symbols for modal operators. Here we will use the box ($\square$) and the diamond ($\lozenge$) for necessity and possibility, respectively, and the fishhook ($\prec$) for strict implication.

[16] See Hughes and Cresswell (1968).

[17] Hughes and Cresswell (1968:25-6).

[18] According to Hughes and Cresswell (1968:30).

[19] Hughes and Cresswell state that S4 and S5 in their (1968) are equivalent to S4 and S5 in Lewis and Langford (1932) but have different bases.

[20] Cf. Hughes and Cresswell (1968: 58). There are still other modal systems; see Hughes and Cresswell (1968:255-273) and (1968:346) for discussion and a diagram illustrating the systems and their relations to one another.

[21] Hughes and Cresswell (1968:47).

[22] The exposition here will be brief and discursive, given the limits of this book. For the comprehensive formal results, see Hughes and Cresswell (1968).

[23] Hughes and Cresswell (1968:49).

[24] Hughes and Cresswell (1968: 43-5).

[25] Hughes and Cresswell (1968: 44).

[26] Hughes and Cresswell (1968:45).

[27] Hughes and Cresswell (1968:50).

[28] Hughes and Cresswell (1968:57-8).

[29] Among others. See for example, Hinktikka (1969); Kanger (1957).

[30] Hughes and Cresswell (1968: 19-20).

[31] See van Heijenoort (1967).

[32] Van Heijenoort (1967).

[33] Not all semantic approaches that make use of possible worlds also use the idea that the truth-value of a modal formula is to be calculated relative to some world (say the actual world); this is a particularity of Kripke's own approach. See Hughes and Cresswell (1968:351).

[34] Note that the situation is just the same for the

symbols of natural language. It is arbitrary that the symbol string 'cat' *means* what it does. Symbol strings do not possess their semantic properties necessarily.

[35] So the remarks in the preface to Kripke (1980) and Kripke (1982) suggest.

2

Naming and Necessity

Introduction

The three lectures given by Saul Kripke at Princeton University in 1970 known as *Naming and Necessity* were given without a written text and without notes (as he adds in a footnote to the 1980 edition, published as a monograph); a remarkable fact, given the content of the lectures. But it is not this alone that resulted in their having become as central as they are to the literature in the philosophy of language today. These three lectures contain one of the severest — and arguably successful — criticisms of a longstanding thesis in the philosophy of language. They also include a number of theses about the meaning and reference of our expressions, what we mean when we talk of the way things might have been, *how* we talk about what might have been; epistemology and metaphysics; the mind-body problem, and a host of other issues central to analytic philosophy.

No one can propose to study the philosophy of language or mind these days without reference to *Naming and Necessity*. No one who *has* studied the philosophy of language can forget coming across, for instance, the concept of rigid designation for the first time; or the meter stick, or the suspicious Schmidt, who might have discovered the incompleteness theorem instead of Gödel; or the speculations as to whether Queen Elizabeth could have been born of other parents...to name just some of the memorable discussions in these lectures.[1] *Naming and Necessity* is more than just a key text; it just about reinvented the way the philosophy of language was done, and, along with other work being done at the time, refashioned the way in which the theory of meaning was examined. The turn of the century saw the

30

birth of analytic philosophy in the work of Frege and Russell; by the end of January of 1970 (when Kripke was about 30 years old), key issues in analytic philosophy were never thought of in the same way again.

Frege: Sense and Reference

What is probably even more remarkable about *Naming and Necessity* is that the topics discussed are not precisely accessible, easy to understand, or even that obviously problematical. The casual and chatty style of the text, moreover, obscures the fact that the issues are complex and technically demanding. So a little background is necessary to highlight Kripke's ideas and place them in context.

At the end of the 19th century, Gottlob Frege (Chapter 1: 5) published a number of books and articles that failed to make a resounding impact on his fellow colleagues in the intellectual community — singularly, given that Frege is now considered the founder of analytic philosophy. But Bertrand Russell came across Frege's work while he was in the midst of producing his three volume *Principia Mathematica* (with his collaborator Alfred North Whitehead), which was devoted to the project of deriving the concepts, laws and principles of mathematics from strictly logical principles.[2] Russell and Frege were to discover that their respective work had this logicist motivation in common, and, in their correspondence, in particular the period from about 1902 through to 1904, we can see the development of some of the fundamental ideas that spawned the shift to analytic philosophy in the 20th century.[3]

Chief among these was a particular thesis about the meaning of expressions. Frege, in a paper sometimes translated as "On Sense and Reference"[4] and now considered the cornerstone of analytic philosophy of language, claimed that the meaning of an expression was the product of two things: what Frege called its *sense* and, in addition, its *reference:* the entity to which the expression referred. Frege did not make the notion of sense completely explicit, but, in general, it has been thought that the *sense* of an expression is meant to provide a *way of determining* the reference, by providing a description or set of descriptions that can be used to identify the object referred to.

Frege himself offers an example like this: consider the center point created by three lines (*a, b,* and *c*) drawn from each angle of an isosceles triangle. We can refer to the very same point in two ways:

The point of intersection of a and b

or

The point of intersection of b and c

Further, and most important, we can create a true identity statement as follows:

The intersection of a and b is identical to the intersection of b with c.

Frege reasoned, on the basis of examples like this one, that the meaning of an expression cannot be its reference alone; if it were, these two expressions would have the same meaning, and the identity statement would be a trivial and obvious one. But they don't have the same meaning, and the identity statement is something we discover, so there must be some other element involved in the meaning of an expression that is used to refer to something like an individual particular thing (like a person, or a mathematical point). Frege called this other element the *sense* of an expression. Frege's claims gave rise to what has become known as the *description theory of meaning*. That is, the way we determine the reference of an expression is by describing it; by setting out characteristics that identify it descriptively and enable us to zero in on the very thing that satisfies the description.

Frege never did argue that these characteristics were *essential* to the object or entity that answered to the description made in those terms, but it was an inevitable consequence of the thesis that this condition was implicitly accepted. We pick out the reference of 'Aristotle,' for instance, by way of descriptions that are to pick him out *uniquely*; so it seems reasonable, if not totally profound, to expect that those descriptions will be by way of his *essential properties*; those characteristics that make him Aristotle and nobody else. As we shall see below, Kripke's criticism of Fregean semantics turns in part on a criticism of this very point.

Now, Frege's thesis is not to be confused with Russell's *theory of descriptions*, although there are points of contact that Kripke exploits in his criticism of what he calls "the Frege-Russell description theory." In brief, the issue concerns the way in which an expression gets its meaning. Either an expression *means* what it *refers to*, or an expression gets its meaning by an intermediate route, such as what Frege called *sense*. Frege defended a theory of *sense* because of certain puzzles that arise with respect to identity statements (later much discussed by Kripke). The example above is one way to frame the problem— here is another:

Hesperus is Phosphorus

Ancient astronomers unwittingly gave two names to the same heavenly body. It was later discovered that the celestial entity referred to as 'Hesperus' was the very same one which was referred to by 'Phosphorus' (the planet Venus, in fact), and a new piece of scientific knowledge was added to the list.

What Frege notes about examples such as these is that the meaning even of what looks like an ordinary proper name cannot be simply the object it refers to; since, again, in this case, the two names 'Hesperus' and 'Phosphorus' would have the same meaning, given that they both refer to the same thing. So what is the meaning of 'Hesperus'? of 'Phosphorus'? Frege can be taken to claim that the meaning of a name (among other referring expressions) is partly construed by its *sense*, which he defines as, again, a way of determining the reference (its 'mode of presentation'). One natural way of determining the reference is by description; on this construal, the name 'Hesperus' is, in effect, a shorter way of saying 'the first body visible in the morning sky,' and the name 'Phosphorus' is a way of saying 'the first body visible in the evening sky.' These descriptions furnish the map, as it were, from the expression — the name — to the object referred to. The idea is, roughly, that with the description in hand, we can go around the world (or, in this case, the sky) and successfully locate the object that matches the description.

One of Frege's most powerful arguments for sense is that what he calls the *informativeness* of an identity statement like the one above must be accounted for, and can't be accounted for, on the view that the meaning of an expression is merely the object it refers to. Suppose that the meaning of 'Hesperus' and that of 'Phosphorus' were simply the very object they refer to. Then it would seem that the truth of the identity statement "Hesperus is Phosphorus" should come as no surprise. After all, it is a metaphysical piece of common sense that an object is identical with itself. If both these expressions have the same reference, and reference is all there is to meaning, then this statement would be one between *synonyms*. It would, in addition, be an example of an analytically true statement; a truth in virtue of meaning alone. Traditionally, these kinds of statements are knowable *a priori* (or independent of experience); and, since no fact about the world is relevant to their truth (only the meanings of the expressions that make it up) then they are also necessarily true.

But the identity statement "Hesperus is Phosphorus" *isn't* known *a priori*. It had to be *discovered,* empirically, to be true. "Hesperus is Phosphorus" is informative; it has what Frege called *cognitive value*.

Compare the sentence "Hesperus is Hesperus." *This* is frankly uninformative about the world of astronomical reality; rather, it tells us a boring fact true about any object (that is identical with itself). It is what is called by a series of philosophers from Locke on down 'trivial' or 'trifling,' or 'merely verbal' — slim to no cognitive value.

Again, if words like 'Hesperus' and 'Phosphorus' get their meaning by way of what they refer to alone, then there should be no difference between the sentences "Hesperus is Hesperus" and "Hesperus is Phosphorus." But there is a difference. And so, Frege proposes his notion of *sense* to account for the difference. Two expressions can have the same *reference*, he argues, but they don't necessarily have to have the same *sense*. There is, in effect, more than one way to determine the reference of an expression; more than one path to a destination. The distinction between sense and reference appears to provide a way to account for the intuitive difference in content between the trivial "Hesperus is Hesperus" and "Hesperus is Phosphorus," which counts as genuine news about something in the world — an advance in our knowledge, and not trivially true.

Now, given that Kripke's lectures are known as *Naming* and *Necessity*, it is worthwhile to point out the status of what is called a 'name' in the philosophy of language. On this there is some difference of opinion. A name, unlike a predicate expression, for instance, or a quantifier, is what is used to pick out an individual particular. There are lots of candidates for this: proper names, pronouns, the word 'here' or the word 'now'; and, controversially, expressions prefixed with the definite article: 'the girl who proposed to my stepson' or 'the unicorn eating grass in the tent.'

Frege, for instance, called all sorts of words 'names.' The group included familiar proper names like 'Hesperus' and 'Aristotle,' and functional or predicate expressions like '___ is red,' as well as whole sentences like "Aristotle was the teacher of Alexander the Great." The distinction between sense and reference applies to everything that Frege called a name, although each sort of 'name' was taken to refer to something different: a proper name referred to an individual; a functional expression referred to a function; and a sentence referred to a truth-value.

But 'naming,' for our purposes, is probably best viewed less technically, and more naturally, as picking out a particular individual thing. Naming is sometimes also called 'referring' or 'denoting,' and, among the philosophical questions raised by the issues of names are, for instance, what *is* a name? How does a name get its meaning? What sort of logical form does a name have? Intuitively, of course, names seem like tags that isolate specific particular things: 'Consuelo' is my name; it seems like the ideal way to pick me out among everybody or everything else. On this view, the meaning of 'Consuelo' is *me*; she who is the bearer of this name. But as we have seen above, the thesis that names just mean what they refer to, and nothing else, raises some puzzles.

Frege considered one of those puzzles, as above, and the upshot of his account is that names are really *descriptive* in content, and the meaning of proper names, at least, do seem to be naturally assessed descriptively. What they refer to is not all that their meaning can consist in. As we shall see next, Russell bequeathed to philosophy another view concerning names and descriptions, though from another angle.[5]

Russell: The Theory of Descriptions

Is this sentence is true or false?:

> The unicorn with the blue stripe on its nose is eating grass on the lawn.

On the face of it, this sentence is false — but in what sense? Is it because the unicorn in question isn't on the lawn, but maybe somewhere else? Isn't eating grass, but maybe a bug instead? Has a black spot and not a blue stripe? Or is it because *there aren't any unicorns*?

Russell's theory of descriptions was, in part, devised to solve this kind of problem. Given that an expression like 'the unicorn' doesn't refer to anything (since there aren't any unicorns), and given the principle that the truth-value of a sentence is a function of the truth-value of its parts, then we are justified in asking what the contribution of an expression like 'the unicorn' really could be in a sentence like "The unicorn with the blue stripe on its nose is eating grass on the lawn." If it's false, *how* is it false?

Something else, equally pressing, is the fact that we *understand* this sentence perfectly well. On the view that says that the meaning of an expression is what it refers to, however, this expression should thus be *meaningless*. But it isn't. So how can we account for its meaning?

Russell's ingenious answer was that *definite descriptions*— that is, expressions of the form 'the *so and so*' — seem to be used to refer to a particular thing (like names do), but it turns out that logically speaking, their role is completely different. In addition to this, Russell claimed that things that *look*, orthographically, like names, aren't mere tags: they are disguised *definite descriptions*. The logical structure and meaning of expressions of the form 'the *so and so*' or a proper name like 'Aristotle' is obscured by the fact that they seem like names, or tags (they occupy the subject place in a sentence, they seem to be used to pick out individual particulars). With the right analysis, however, we can uncover their genuine logical and semantic content.

The theory of descriptions works as follows. A sentence containing a definite description such as:

>The present King of France is bald

is analyzed as:

>At least one thing is present King of France
>
>At most one thing is present King of France
>
>And that thing is bald [6]

That is, the sentence "The present king of France is bald" is, logically speaking, an existentially quantified sentence, which, in effect, makes a claim that can be far more easily assessed as true or false. Either there is, or there is not, a particular unique object that answers to the description specified. If there is nothing that satisfies this description, the sentence is false. There is, in fact, nothing that does satisfy this description, and so, the sentence is straightforwardly false.

Between Frege and Russell's theses about names and their meaning there are many points of contact, but also some genuine differences. Russell, for instance, found that Frege's notion of *sense* interfered with knowledge of the world, and maintained the view to the contrary that the meaning of an expression just was (ultimately) what it referred to. Of course, this led to some puzzles,[7] among which was the puzzle concerning expressions that *had* no reference and what they meant, and how; and thus was born the theory of descriptions. Frege's thesis, on the other hand, does seem to give a descriptive theory of sense some priority. In short, the issue of naming and describing is one that plays a significant role in both Frege's and Russell's theories of meaning, even though the details pertaining to each theory, and the motivations that lie behind each one differ. It is with respect to the issue of naming and describing, however, and the meaning of a name, that Kripke launches an attack on what he calls "the Frege-Russell description theory." We turn to this next.

Rigid Designation

Kripke begins *Naming and Necessity* by hoping his audience "sees some connection between the two topics" that make up the title of the lectures (1980: 22). But it must be said that the connection is not immediately obvious. The idea, as Kripke argues in Lecture I, is that there are modal considerations that can be raised about the reference of name that show that the meaning of a name is not descriptive.[8] Ultimately, Kripke does not offer a positive account of the meaning of a proper name, but his arguments against their descriptive content have become definitive in the literature.

What Kripke exploits in his criticism of what he calls the "Frege-Russell description theory" is modality, as discussed in Chapter 1, above. In particular, what Kripke does is to ask about what might *have been true* about the object referred to by the name in other possible worlds. It turns out that posing modal questions about what might have been true of, say, Clinton, makes a description theory of the meaning of names like 'Clinton' appear to run aground.

If a description theory of the meaning of a name is correct, then 'Clinton' means (to choose a description that picks out the reference of that name uniquely), 'the man elected president of the United States in 1992.' Now, surely Clinton might not have been elected president; it all could have gone some other way. So there is a possible world in which *our* Clinton — ex-governor of Arkansas, girl-watcher, father of one — is not the person that will answer to the description 'the man elected president of the United States in 1992.' But if that is so, Kripke asks, how can we ever talk about what might have happened (or not) to *Clinton*? In a possible world in which it isn't our Clinton that got to be president, that description picks out another person. But we don't want to talk about the *other* person when we talk about what might have happened to Clinton. So how can we refer to *Clinton* in counterfactual situations? That is, given that the sentence 'Clinton might not have been elected president' makes sense, how does it do so?

Kripke's answer is that a proper name like 'Clinton' is a *rigid designator*, defined as an expression that refers to the same object in all possible worlds. In contrast, the expression 'The man elected president of the United States in 1992' is not a rigid designator, because it refers to *whoever* was elected president of the United States in 1992, in some possible world — Wayne Gretzky, say, in the possible world where Gretzky runs for president. What Kripke claims here is that it is perfectly legitimate to wish to speak of, and to successfully speak of, counterfactual situations with respect to one and the same object. But if so, then the meaning of a name cannot be an associated description, because, as his examples show, a name and a description behave differently in counterfactual situations; each delivers a different reference. Hence, Kripke argues, there must be a semantic difference between a name and a description — the meaning of a name cannot be descriptive.

One crucial point that Kripke makes is that natural counterfactual discourse makes it important to account for how we talk about the *same* object in different possible worlds. In particular, what we *don't* want to say is what would have happened to some *counterpart* of Clinton, when we say 'Clinton might not have been elected president.' Counterpart theory, transworld identification, and essentialism, all discussed briefly but searingly by Kripke in the *Naming and Necessity* lectures, were among the number of themes that came to be discussed in detail in the years to follow. We make a few comments on these next.

Counterpart Theory and Transworld Identification

A common criticism of the concept of rigid designation is that it begs the question concerning reference to an object in a counterfactual situation (a situation where things are different than they are in the actual world). The criticism goes like this: How do we know that we are referring to *Aristotle* even when we use 'Aristotle' as a rigid designator? How do we — how *can* we — identify Aristotle *himself* in a possible world where he has none of the properties he has in the actual world (where he is, for instance, a hockey player or an electrician)? After all, don't we identify Aristotle by a set of descriptions that presumably pick him out from among everybody else, according to his unique characteristics (how else do we know it's *him*)? In the possible world(s) where he doesn't have any of those characteristics, how can we find him? On this view, either Aristotle has essential properties (making rigid designation unnecessary), or we have to refer to him by description (putting us back where we started).

There is, in fact, a longstanding dispute that acts as background to this sort of criticism that is worthwhile to mention briefly here. From about the late 1940s (when Ruth Barcan Marcus began publishing her work on quantified modal logic) on through to the 1970s, W.V.O. Quine published a series of influential papers criticizing what he called *essentialism*. This is the notion, as he sees it, that necessity applies not just to sentences, but also the way in which an object might possess a property. This sort of view flies in the face of any stringent nominalist/positivist framework, (with its emphasis on empiricist principles of verification for knowledge, and of the bare minimum in metaphysical entities) of which Quine is a contemporary canonical exemplar.

Kripke in fact refers to Quine's well-known counterexample to the view that particulars could have essential properties. In brief, the claim is that any attempt to attribute a so-called essential or necessary property to a particular will depend on how the particular is described or referred to. But then, if the possession of what is supposed to be a necessary property turns on such an arbitrary verbal distinction, the whole notion of a necessary property seems subject to doubt. For instance, to say that "Necessarily nine is nine" is to make a standard identity statement, where necessity plays the role of a linguistic operator on the sentence 'nine is nine.' Now, there are nine planets in our solar system. So the sentence:

Nine is the number of planets

is a true sentence. But what happens when we replace the first occurrence of the expression 'nine' in the first example sentence with an expression that *also* refers to the number nine? We get the following:

Necessarily, the number of planets is nine.

But this is, of course, false. There didn't have to be nine planets in our solar system, there could have been any number. So, according to Quine, a necessity operator introduces a context that can lead to failure of substitutivity of co-referential terms. A sentence prefixed by a necessity operator may not retain its truth-value when co-referential terms ('nine,' 'the number of planets') are substituted one for the other. So, as Quine sees, it, essentialism is called into doubt. So-called necessary properties seem to be a question of how something is described, and evaporate under another description.

This issue of essentialism was fought over in detail in the years following the formalization of quantificational modal logic,[9] and in itself, spawn problems only indirectly related to the concept of rigid designation. But Kripke himself notes that the topic of essentialism is relevant to the issues he is discussing: it is, he says, "related to the view that the way we refer to particular things is by a description" (1980: 40). In fact, Kripke's point is that Quine's criticism simply highlights the difference between a rigid designator ('nine') and a non-rigid designator ('the number of planets').

According to Kripke, any criticism of the notion of rigid designation from something like Quine's anti-essentialist perspective is based on a confusion about the notion of counterfactual discourse. The issue is not that an object has necessary properties *only* by description, so that an attempt to refer to *that* object in counterfactual situations will fail, and that rigid designation begs the question with respect to reference by description. Rather, Kripke claims (1980: 44), we must keep in mind that we do *not* look at another possible world "through a telescope," observing independently existing particulars and their properties, and looking for, say, Aristotle— but without any of the (allegedly essential) properties we associate with him in the actual world. Rather, Kripke claims, our counterfactual discourse involves *stipulating* a possible world; one drawn up according to the specifications we require: "given by the descriptive conditions we associate with it" (1980: 44). We determine what it is that we wish to refer to by a description that singles it out in the actual world, and go on to talk about *it* in counterfactual situations.

What we must realize, as Kripke sees it, is that it is ultimately irrelevant that a given description may hold of the object *only* in the actual world. To talk about whether *Aristotle* could have been an electrician, and not the greatest philosopher of antiquity, we need merely to *fix the reference* of the name by a description or set of descriptions that apply to our Aristotle and which deliver the man in question. Once we have done so, we are free to discuss what *might have happened to* him. Any other view, Kripke claims, has the undesirable consequence that we can't talk about what might have been the case about *Aristotle* himself, but, instead, of some *counterpart* of Aristotle. But, again, in counterfactual discourse we are presumably not interested in what someone sort of like Aristotle, but not Aristotle, might or might not have accomplished; we want to talk about *Aristotle*. According to Kripke, only a notion of rigid designation can do the job.

Kripke's position here turns on an important criticism he makes of the notion of Fregean sense. One of the most important distinctions to come out of *Naming and Necessity* is that a description can be and often is used to do what Kripke calls 'fix the reference' of an expression, rather than give its meaning (act as a synonym, for instance). What Kripke argues is that Fregean sense is proposed — illegitimately — as a semantic element that plays *both* roles, but without sufficient distinction between those roles made plain. The distinction emerges clearly in one of Kripke's most well known examples, the case of the meter stick, as we will see below.

Descriptions: Fixing Reference vs. Giving Meaning

Kripke begins by suggesting the following: suppose we stipulate that the length of certain stick *S* in the actual world will be referred to by the expression 'one meter.' The question Kripke asks is whether the sentence:

Stick *S* is one meter long

is necessarily true. Now, it is true that while Kripke uses this example to highlight the difference between an expression that is a rigid designator and one that is not. But it is important to note that from this example emerged, as well, another distinction that is one of the most notable in *Naming and Necessity*: the distinction between metaphysical necessity and epistemological necessity, as we will see shortly.[10]

Suppose we stipulate that the length in our world, of a certain stick, stick *S*, will be used as a descriptive definition of the expression 'one meter.' What Kripke asks is whether the sentence "Stick *S* is one meter long" is necessarily true, as it would have to be, if 'the length of stick *S*' was meant to be a synonym for the expression 'one meter.' Kripke denies this, however, by arguing that 'the length of stick *S* ' is a non-rigid designator, which picks out *whatever* length stick *S* happens to be in whatever possible world contains stick *S*. What this means is that 'stick *S* is one meter long' is not, after all necessarily true, since it might not be that *that* is the length of stick *S* in every possible world.

What is the case, however, is that the description 'the length of stick *S*' can be plausibly considered as employed in *fixing the reference* of the expression 'one meter,' and, what's more, fixing it such that the expression 'one meter' rigidly designates *that* very length in every possible world. What we use the actual length of stick *S* in the actual world to do, according to Kripke, is to furnish a descriptive definition of the expression that we wish to use in the actual world — 'one meter.' In the actual world, stick *S* is length L, whatever that length may be (the length, Kripke says (1980: 76), was supposed to be "the distance when the arm of King Henry I of England was outstretched from the tip of his finger to his nose."). The length stick *S* has in the actual world is an accidental property of Stick *S*; Stick *S* could have any length at all. But once we fix the reference of 'one meter' by *that* length, the expression 'one meter' becomes a rigid designator that picks out *that* length in every possible world.

This example enabled Kripke to make some interesting remarks that could be said to have changed the way that the concept of necessity was considered in analytic philosophy from that time forward. A few basics are in order, however, to understand the issue clearly.

Epistemological and Metaphysical Necessity

Philosophy has embraced, at least since Kant and Locke and perhaps even before, a distinction, broadly speaking, between truth in virtue of meaning (analytic truth) and truth in virtue of the world (synthetic truth). Analytic truth has traditionally been conceived as truth between synonyms. A sentence like:

41

Bachelors are unmarried men

is a canonical example of an analytic truth; the sentence is true because of a relation between the meanings of its component words. By contrast, a sentence like:

This room has no bachelors in it

is true, if it's true, only if the world is as it is depicted by the component words; only if it's true that this room has no bachelors in it, but only women, priests, widowers, children, and/or married men. Now, the distinction between analytic and synthetic sentences (or, more accurately, propositions) has long been the subject of controversy, but, in general, each type of sentence has had distinct properties associated with it.

Analytic propositions are generally classified as those known *a priori* (by virtue of reason alone; by virtue of meaning alone; without investigation into or evidence culled from the world), and, concomitantly, necessarily true or false (since the world at large does not play a role in establishing them as true or false their truth value will not change). Synthetic propositions are those that are known, by contrast, through investigation or empirical evidence; that is, they are known *a posteriori*. As a result, their truth-value is considered contingent, and not necessary, since matters in the world that correspond to a particular synthetic sentence could change, taking the truth-value of the sentence along with it. In the example above, for instance, this room could suddenly get some bachelors in it, and the sentence would no longer be true.

The reasons that historically lie behind the pairing of necessity and aprioricity to analytic sentences are complex, but they appear to stem from a particular assumption about meaning, and the theory of meaning. This assumption can be generally characterized as one that claims that the meaning of our expressions is substantively different in kind from the world of objects and properties that are referred to by expressions that we use. Not that there is no intuitive basis for such a view (known as *internalism* in the philosophical literature). We do not have actual objects *in our heads* when we think and talk about them. What we do have is some sort of mental representation; and it is the metaphysical character of mental representation, and views thereof, that governs this issue.

Internalism is the view that since nothing outside the psychological subject's physical confines need affect the content of his mental states, nothing outside the mind *determines* or individuates the content of our mental states (makes them what they are). Whatever

42

mental concepts are, or mental content is, or mental representation is (these are more or less different ways of saying the same thing), they will not essentially involve the things that are represented *by* the mind itself in any theory of *its* nature.

The basis for this view is Cartesian. Descartes (among others) took the view that the content of a mental state such as belief could be what it is quite independent of the way things were with the *objects* of the belief. One may possess the belief that outside the window there are people walking dogs, without that belief being *true*. The falsity of the belief, however, won't change the *nature* of that belief; to wit, that it is the *belief that outside the window people are walking dogs* (and not the belief that frogs are falling from the sky, say). From this fact about mental representation an internalist theory of meaning was born, which, ultimately, served to obscure much about the topics of necessity, *a priori*, and the analytic, as Kripke did so much to show.[11]

One of Kripke's greatest contributions in *Naming and Necessity* — and to philosophy itself — was to point out that, notwithstanding the traditional pairing of the *a priori* with the necessary, and the complementary pairing of the *a posteriori* with the contingent, in fact, these concepts lie along entirely different philosophical planes. The necessary and the contingent, Kripke points out, are *metaphysical* concepts; they govern considerations about the way the world is. The *a priori* and the *a posteriori* are *epistemological* ones; they govern considerations about the way in which we acquire knowledge.

Historical tradition to the contrary, thus, there is no reason why there couldn't be a necessary *a posteriori* truth; nor any reason why there couldn't be a contingent *a priori* truth. The trick is to find convincing examples to demonstrate it. The example concerning the length of stick *S* was briefly discussed by Kripke as being an example of, in fact, a contingent *a priori* truth. But it is safe to say one of the most permanent changes to the philosophical landscape in the last 30 years was due, in part, to Kripke's discussion of *a posteriori* necessity. We turn to this next.

The Semantics of Natural Kind Terms

Kripke's views about the semantics of *common* nouns are an example of what became known as *semantic externalism* in the philosophical literature. Along with Hilary Putnam's article 'Meaning and Reference,'[12] the view sometimes called 'The New Theory of Reference' was introduced to philosophy, which changed the way the theory of meaning was pursued. Both Kripke and Putnam refer to the other in their work; here we can elucidate the main lines of argument for externalism.[13]

The sorts of examples Kripke uses to put the view across are effected by what are known as *natural kind terms*. These are common nouns that pick out natural categories of things: 'tiger,' 'gold,' and 'water,' for instance (the view, however, has been extended to all terms in the ensuing years).[14] It is customary to understand the basics along the lines of Putnam's so-called 'Twin Earth' examples, as follows.

Twin Earth

How do we establish the meaning of a term like 'water'? The Fregean method is to associate a number of descriptive concepts with the term 'water;' 'tasteless,' 'transparent,' 'liquid,' for instance. The substance that answers to those descriptions (the set of them, perhaps),[15] is water. In addition, given that Fregean sense can be defined as the way of determining the reference, there can be no two terms with the same *sense* but a different reference (too much ambiguity if so). What uniquely answers the description in question is the reference of the term in question.

But now suppose that there exists a possible world out there (call it Twin Earth) where everything is a molecular duplicate of what it is on Earth, except the substance that falls from the skies and fills the lakes and rivers (as Putnam puts it). That stuff has a chemical formula that isn't H_2O, like it is on earth; it's complicated, so it's abbreviated as XYZ. On Twin Earth they use the term 'water' — spelled the same, pronounced the same — to refer to XYZ. The question that arises now is this: what does 'water' mean? Clearly 'tasteless, colorless liquid' picks out XYZ on Twin Earth, but H_2O on Earth. So the descriptive set of concepts associated with the term 'water' both on Twin Earth and Earth determine *different* substances. This flies in the face of the Fregean dictum that two terms could not have the same sense and pick out a different reference. As Putnam sets up the Twin Earth example, the same set of descriptions, correlated to the same *word* water, pick out two different things. So what can 'water' mean? H_2O? XYZ? Both? Given this ambiguity, we have to ask: is the meaning of 'water' really a set of descriptions? Or does the very substance picked out to enter into an analysis of the meaning of the term?

Putnam claims the very substance that the respective terms refer to — H_2O on Earth and XYZ on Twin Earth — *does* contribute to the meaning of 'water'; so that word does *not* have the same meaning on Earth as it does on Twin Earth. The way Kripke puts it, of course, is to say that the word 'water' is a *rigid designator*, but that the description 'tasteless colorless liquid' is not.

44

Now, the issue Kripke highlights is the status of the identity statement:

Water is H_2O.

According to Kripke, this statement is necessary, but it is known through empirical investigation, so it is *a posteriori.* What makes it a necessary truth? It isn't that 'H_2O' is a synonym for 'water' — the Twin Earth example establishes that whatever else the description 'substance whose chemical formula is H_2O' is doing, it is not *giving the meaning* of the term 'water.' What makes it a necessary truth, according to Kripke, is that both 'water' and 'H_2O' are rigid designators; so the sentence 'water is H_2O' must always be true.

One way to see this is to note that the metaphysical situation with respect to natural kind terms and the like is such that an *appearance-reality* distinction is at work.[16] The nature of water is established by its chemical composition, not how it appears to our senses. But semantic common sense dictates that what the term 'water' refers to has to appeal to what water *is*, or there would be ambiguity: the description picks out XYZ on Twin Earth, and who knows what else in other possible worlds. Things, after all, can *look* otherwise than what they are (and be described accordingly). But our semantic theory must not be fooled by appearances.

Not only did the concept of rigid designation give us a plausible way of analyzing our talk about modality, it also enabled Kripke to make a profound and telling point against centuries of philosophical tradition concerning the necessary and the *a priori*. From Kripke's point that there is a difference between the way the world is and the way it contributes to our knowledge he is able to derive a substantive difference between epistemological necessity and metaphysical necessity. Of the many remarkable philosophical points in *Naming and Necessity* it is fair to say that this one has had the longest-lasting impact. A number of distinctions that have occupied a central role at the heart of analytic philosophy have had to be reconsidered because of it: the *de re/de dicto* distinction, and the analytic/synthetic distinction, to name just two.[17] Further, as we will see below, what Kripke ultimately argues is that *all* true identity statements between rigid designators will be *necessarily* true, a claim he exploits against the identity theory about the mind and the body, a central thesis in 20th century philosophy of mind. Before tracing the far-reaching consequences of the distinction, however, we must return briefly to some remaining details of Kripke's criticism of the "Frege-Russell description theory," and his positive view about the meaning of a name.

45

A 'Better Picture'

Lecture II of *Naming and Necessity* begins with a summary of the "Frege-Russell" description theory, which Kripke presents as six theses and one condition on the satisfaction of those theses. The condition is that the theory cannot be *circular*. That is, 'the description theory' is a theory of reference, and so cannot help itself to a notion of reference that isn't in some way independently specified. We can begin with the first of the six theses (Kripke 1980: 71):

> (1) To every name or designating expression 'X', there corresponds a cluster of properties, namely the family of those properties φ such A believes 'φ X.'

That is, as Kripke notes, the so-called description theory is not necessarily the theory that reference is established by *one* uniquely relevant and fitting description of the object in question. Rather, it is more plausible (and he cites various defenders of this view)[18] that a description theory of naming makes use of a *family* or *cluster* of descriptions to pick out the reference of the name in question. What the object is described as having, of course, is a family or cluster of certain *properties*, which, as Kripke sees it, are both believed by a speaker to be possessed by the object, and:

> (2) [...] are believed by a speaker to pick out some individual uniquely.

In addition:

> (3) If most, or a weighted most, of the φ's are satisfied by one unique object *y*, then *y* is the referent of 'X.'

Moreover:

> (4) If the vote yields no unique object, 'X' does not refer.

There are two more theses that add a more substantive philosophical overlay to the 'description theory,' as Kripke summarizes it:

> (5) The statement, 'If X exists, then X has most of the φ's' is known *a priori* by the speaker.

> (6) The statement 'If X exists, then X has most of the φ's' expresses a necessary truth (in the idiolect of the speaker).

The first point to clarify is the claim that the description theory is better defended by way of a cluster of properties held to be possessed by a putative object of reference, something that Kripke denies with effective use of examples. As Kripke shows, whether or not the

46

descriptions used to determine an object of reference are one or are many, the result is that a seemingly indefensible situation will arise with respect to the truth of the statements those descriptions generate.

To begin with, if the reference of 'Aristotle' is he who answers the description — who possesses the property — 'the teacher of Alexander,' then this suggests that the sentence 'Aristotle was the teacher of Alexander' is a necessary truth. The property, that is, is one believed by a speaker to be uniquely and necessarily possessed by *Aristotle*. But, of course, Aristotle might well have been no one's teacher. Being Alexander's teacher is not, in fact, a necessary or essential property of Aristotle, so 'Aristotle was the teacher of Alexander' is not necessarily true.

Given this, defenders of the view claim that it is more plausible instead to attribute to the reference of 'Aristotle' some group or cluster of properties, which can be claimed, even disjunctively, for the object referred to by the name. The group, or a significant number of the group of properties, will be the determinants of the referent. On this sort of view, then, it is whoever is *F* or *G* or *H* that is picked out by the name 'Aristotle.'[19]

But Kripke denies this, by wielding in his criticism of the cluster theory what is, in effect, the same point noted above in the context of transworld identification. There just isn't, he claims, any good reason to suppose that Aristotle had *any* of the properties commonly associated with him, let alone *necessarily*. Stacking properties up in clusters, even disjunctive clusters, doesn't help. One of the first ways in which the description theory goes wrong, according to Kripke, is where it claims that the attribution of properties to the object referred to by a name attributes any of those properties to the object *necessarily*.

Having argued against thesis (6), as above, Kripke goes on to ask, "what picture of naming do theses (1)-(5) give you?" And, he says, the picture is this: "You give some condition which uniquely determines an object, and you use a certain word as a name for the object determined by this condition" (1980:79). But, as he will argue, in most cases, the theses — and the picture that lies behind them — appear to be false.

Thesis (2), for instance, asserts that reference is achieved in part by a property or some cluster of them that is believed by the speaker to pick out an individual uniquely. But what Kripke asserts, on the contrary, is that we *can* (indeed, *do*) refer to (for instance) the physicist Richard Feynman, even if the only description on offer is 'a famous physicist.' Kripke's argument, elaborated in his positive theory of naming, turns on the intuitive claim that even when we *can't* offer a description any more uniquely specifying than 'a physicist' to refer to Richard Feynman, we may, all the same, genuinely refer to Feynman by using the name 'Feynman.' This is because, according to Kripke, the act of naming or referring as depicted by the description theory is flawed; and there is a better picture. What establishes the reference of a name, Kripke claims, is a link from the object designated by a name to the rest of the community (1980: 91):

> … the name is spread from link to link as if by a chain. A speaker who is on the far end of this chain, who has heard about, say, Richard Feynman, in the market place or elsewhere, may be referring to Richard Feynman….A certain passage of communication reaching ultimately to the man himself does reach the speaker. He is then referring to Feynman even though he can't identify him uniquely.

Kripke's positive view about naming stands behind his rejection of Thesis (3), which he accomplishes with an example that has become standard citation in the literature. Thesis (3) claims that the reference of a name is that unique object that satisfies the property or cluster of properties attributed by the speaker. But, Kripke asks, is this really so? Suppose it turns out that a mysterious Schmidt is the person who in fact discovered the incompleteness of arithmetic, and not Gödel, who gets the credit for the discovery. On the picture painted by the description theory, according to Kripke, when we use the name 'Gödel' we are, in fact, referring to *Schmidt*, since Schmidt is the one who answers to the uniquely specifying description 'he who discovered the incompleteness of arithmetic.' But does referring to an individual really amount to being merely the end result delivered by a particular description?

Kripke says no. It is just counterintuitive, he says, that we refer to this Schmidt rather than to Gödel when we use the name 'Gödel,' *even if* Schmidt is the one who satisfies the descriptions we employ, believing we are picking out *Gödel* uniquely. Instead, Kripke claims, what establishes reference to Gödel is the actual chain of communication from Gödel himself to the speakers in the community that use a name to refer to him (1980: 95):

> In general our reference depends not just on what we think ourselves, but on other people in the community, the history of how a name reached one, and things like that. It is by following such a history that one gets to the reference.

Kripke's positive view of naming is offered in explicit opposition to what he calls a certain 'picture' of reference that stands behind the description theory. Challenge the picture, he argues, and you challenge the theory. The picture, as Kripke represents it, is one that proposes that naming is achieved by what he characterizes as a solitary, private, mental ceremony. In this 'ceremony,' we assert or decree that who or what the name names will be who or what is the only thing that possesses certain identifying properties. But a different picture is the correct one, Kripke claims: we refer to a certain person, say, by virtue of a connection with other members of our linguistic community, *including* the person we wish to refer to by a name.

Now, as we argued above, Kripke's defense of semantic externalism can be understood by way of appearance-reality distinction, a distinction which is plausible for terms like 'water' or 'gold.' What establishes the reference of 'water,' according to externalism, is *not* a description based on the *perceptual* qualities of a particular substance ('tasteless, colorless, liquid'), but turns instead on what water *is* (the chemical compound H_2O). What we can do here is extend this point to help clarify Kripke's positive view about naming.

Recall that Kripke was able to show by way of example that the property or properties that may uniquely specify *Aristotle* (for instance) in the actual world ('the greatest philosopher of antiquity'; 'the student of Plato') will not necessarily pick out the *same man* in another possible world. Almost any set of so-called uniquely specifying properties can be rigged to pick out another object in another possible world; too many things, that is, can look like essential properties that turn out not to be, thus losing us consistency of reference throughout other possible worlds.

Extending the appearance/reality analogy to the issue of the reference of proper names merely requires that we look at the case of naming by way of the historical philosophical distinction between *accidental/contingent* properties and *essential* properties. What we can say, plausibly, is that sets of attributed properties — even if believed to be uniquely specifying and essential to a particular individual — can in fact turn out to be contingently possessed by that individual. Aristotle didn't *have to be* the greatest philosopher of antiquity, or the student of Plato; these are properties that *he* — that very man — could shed in another possible world. But what he can't shed, of course, is the property of being identical with *himself*. What we refer to, when we use the name 'Aristotle,' is *him*; not a possessor of what turn out to be contingent properties, whoever he may be.

Recall that, according to Kripke, we must not mistake the *role* of a description in the process of naming and reference. A description can be used to *fix the reference* of a name like 'Aristotle,' but once we have so fixed it, then what we have created is a *rigid designator* (as discussed above). A proper name like 'Aristotle,' as a rigid designator, will pick out *that very man* in *every* possible world.

What Kripke further asserts is that what makes *Aristotle* (the man) the referent of the name 'Aristotle,' is a history of reference to a particular person with that name. The reference is established first by those in closest proximity to him, and then in ever widening circles, passed on from speaker to speaker in the community. What we avoid, on this view, is the claim that the description gives the *meaning* of the name.

Kripke in fact uses the term 'baptism' to elaborate his positive view (1980: 96):

> A rough statement of a theory might be the following: An initial 'baptism' takes place. Here the object may be named by ostension, or the reference of the name may be fixed by a description. When the name is 'passed from link to link,' the receiver of the name must, I think, intend when he learns it to use it with the same reference as the man from whom he heard it.

Now, Kripke is candid enough to claim that his positive view assumes a notion of 'intending' to use the same reference as others in the community (1980: 97), about which he offers nothing in the way of explicit or detailed argument. And he does admit that he has fallen short of offering a theory of reference or naming, if that means specifying necessary and sufficient conditions for reference to an object. His concern, he claims, was to offer a better picture of what reference consists of than the picture offered by the description theorists. And, he says, he thinks he has done so (1980: 97).

For the most part, of course, the philosophical literature has agreed with him; *Naming and Necessity* had an enormous impact on theories of meaning and reference in analytic philosophy. In the next section, however, we will note some of the criticisms that have been brought to bear on certain aspects of Kripke's position. In particular, we can focus on a specific issue that arises with respect to the connection between names and necessity (and that can serve by way of introduction to the subject of Lecture III): identity statements between names, and their modal character.

Names and Necessity: Some Critical Comments

One issue that has been raised (see, for instance, Dummett 1972)[20] is whether Kripke is faithful or accurate to either Frege or Russell with respect to what he calls 'the description theory.' The criticism here is that it is difficult to find any explicit commitment in Frege or Russell to (for example) a solitary, private, mental ceremony by which we decree that the reference of a name N shall be the unique particular that satisfies a description D that Kripke attributes to 'the description theory.' Moreover, one could claim with some plausibility that Frege never claims that his notion of sense is meant to be *both* a reference-fixer *and* a meaning-conferrer for an expression; Frege is notoriously inexact about what a notion of sense really amounts to. [21]

The concept of rigid designation itself is not entirely without controversy either. In particular, the question arises as to whether *only* names are rigid designators; whether there is some unique modal characteristic about names that other referring expressions, similar in logical role to names, don't share. Since proper names, after all, are only one of a wider set of referring expressions logically known as *singular terms* (terms that purport to pick out or refer to an individual particular), then we can ask whether other singular terms can't be rigid designators, too. Rigid designators, as we saw above, are modally defined: a rigid designator is an expression that refers to the same particular in *all* possible worlds. Given Kripke's assertion that we can fix *the reference* of a name by stipulation, and go on to stipulate that the name will refer to the same object in every possible world, then there doesn't seem to be much standing in the way of doing so for any other sort of singular term. We could even do it for definite descriptions. We fix the reference of the definite description 'the oldest structure in Rome' by stipulation as follows: 'the oldest structure in Rome *in the actual world.*' What is there now to prevent us using that definite description to refer to the same building in all possible worlds? We have fixed its reference by way of an accidental property — the age of the oldest structure in Rome in the actual world — but once we have done so, we have created an expression — a rigid designator — that refers to the same structure in all possible worlds.

It could also be argued, on the heels of the above point, that there is nothing *specifically* about names, as referring expressions, that generate the modal puzzles about reference that Kripke emphasizes; other referring expressions might well generate similar puzzles. In addition, there is a question that arises about the *kind* of modal puzzle that Kripke claims that names generate. We saw in Chapter 1 that there is a difference between *de re* necessity (the necessary possession of a property by a particular) and *de dicto* necessity (the attribution of necessary truth to a sentence/proposition). Kripke's points about what properties might or might not have been possessed by a particular individual in another possible world — whose broader role is played in an argument that names cannot be descriptive in content — appear to speak to necessity *de re* ('of the thing'). But the question is: is there really a connection between names and *de re* necessity? If a particular has a property necessarily it is hard to see how, or in what way, a linguistic entity — a name (or other singular term) — will impinge on that fact.

Finally there is the issue of identity statements between names, the focus of Lecture III of *Naming and Necessity*. What Kripke will argue, in the course of a series of attacks on a certain theory about mind-body identity, is that identity statements between names are necessary. This point turns on names being rigid designators, but, as we have mentioned above, if it turns out that other expressions can be rigid designators as well, then there is no special connection between names and necessary identity statements; the emphasis Kripke places on names is might be overstated.

These issues continue to be discussed, 30 years after Kripke gave the *Naming and Necessity* lectures (a testament to their impact on contemporary philosophy). But *Naming and Necessity* also contains a discussion of one of the most central topics in 20th century philosophy: the mind-body problem. In particular, Kripke makes a series of points against the thesis of mind-body identity, or 'the identity theory,' as it sometimes known. He adds, along the way, some definitive remarks on the topic of essential properties and the critical importance of the distinction between epistemological properties and metaphysical ones. We turn to Lecture III next.

Mind-Body Identity and Rigid Designation

Lecture III of *Naming and Necessity* contains, among other things, a definitive criticism of the mind-body identity thesis, a cornerstone of 20th century philosophy of mind. This thesis has various formulations, but in general, the thesis claims that dualism is, in fact, incorrect — the mind is not metaphysically distinct from the body. The motivation for this sort of view is not a weak one. Our best and most successful scientific theories about the nature of reality are materialist. To sanction an entity, metaphysically distinct in kind from the body or the brain, would be to have to admit that our physical theories are inadequate to capture the nature of the mind. To sanction such an entity in spite of that, however, would raise the insurmountable problem of mind-body interaction; if the mind and the body really are metaphysically distinct in kind, and the mind isn't material, then how can there be any causal interaction between the two? But isn't there?

Considerations such as these have given materialism about the mind predominance in 20th theories of the nature of mind. But Kripke brings together a number of the points he develops in *Naming and Necessity* to deny the materialist identity thesis. Kripke's strategy is to claim that an identity statement, will be *necessarily* true, if true, if the statement is made by way of expressions that are rigid designators. And what Kripke will show is that the expressions used in canonical mind-body identity statements are rigid designators, but the identity statement is false.

Identity

The issue here comprises a number of topics, which we can begin to explain by way of background. We can start with identity, and go on to explore necessity, synonymy, analyticity, and the *a priori* in its wake.

A notable question in philosophy has been known to arise over the sort of relation identity is meant to be. As Kripke himself notes, even Frege, at one time, was tempted to defend identity as a relation that applies to *expressions* rather than to objects themselves.[22] Two expressions that are said to be identical are so, presumably, from having the same meaning. But then, as Frege noted, the question arises as to what their meaning consists in. As we saw above, if the meaning of an expression is simply what it refers to, then there should be no difference between, for example, the identity statement

> Tom Cruise is Tom Cruise
>
> and
>
> Tom Cruise is Thomas Mopather

given that the expressions 'Tom Cruise' and 'Thomas Mopather ' refer to the same person. We should be able to read off the truth of the second in the same way as we do the first — *a priori*. We should classify the truth of the second statement as necessary, like we do the first. After all, if the meaning of an expression is just what it refers to, then there should be no difference between these two statements. But there is; and in order to explain this, Frege, as we saw above, abandoned the view that identity was a relation between expressions, and captured the cognitive difference between two statements of identity as in the examples above by way of the distinction between sense and reference.

Now, identity, statements of identity, and the semantic character of statements of identity have taken center stage in the contemporary philosophical literature on the mind-body problem. One of the most notable confusions in the philosophical literature for a long time was that of the assumption that an identity statement *had* to be about expressions, given that the truth of the statement could vary given variation in the way objects were referred to. Identity and synonymy thus were linked; but the issue of synonymy was an issue about meaning, about which many philosophers had either nominalist doubts or internalist presuppositions. Kripke makes it clear, however, that the relation he is interested in exploring is precisely that of identity considered as a metaphysical relation that every object holds to itself. But the first thing he has to argue against is the view that certain kinds of identities are contingently true.

One of the earliest views to make this explicit was in a paper by the Australian philosopher J.J.C. Smart called 'Sensations and Brain Processes.'[23] Smart argues there for materialism as the correct view of the mind-body problem, claiming that the statement

Sensations = brain processes

is a genuine statement of identity, even though it was an empirical discovery that sensations and brain processes are correlated (or more). The *word* 'sensation' and the *word* 'brain process' are not synonyms, to be sure. The statement is not analytic; it is not necessarily true or known *a priori*. The identity claim is thus said to be contingent and informative — it is discovered that we are referring to the same thing two different ways — and known *a posteriori*, but it is, Smart claims, a genuine identity. This position is taken to be a foundational attempt to establish materialism about the mind once and for all, partly based on the analogy between mind-body identity and other theoretical identities, held to be similar in kind, with which materialism is defended. The issue, from which we can better understand Kripke's line of argument (among other things) will turn on whether contingent identities can be realistically defended for the issue of mind-body identity.

Necessary and Contingent Identities

It seems that the use of descriptions in a purported identity statement can unproblematically generate a contingent identity. Kripke cites the following example (1980: 98): "The man who invented bifocals was the first Postmaster General of the United States," as a straightforward contingent identity, in that it is perfectly possible that whoever invented bifocals need not have been the first Postmaster General of the United States. So, Kripke claims, when you make a statement to the effect that a particular described in one way and a particular described in another way are one and the same, "that can be a contingent fact" (1980: 98). Identity statements made with descriptions such as these, Kripke would say, are composed of *non-rigid* designators, and are contingently true.

The case of identity statements between names, however, has raised some controversy. As cited by Kripke, at least, there is no definitive consensus about how to classify identity statements involving names. For instance is

Cicero = Tully

a necessary truth? The arguments against this involve the longstanding historical conflation of the concepts of necessity, analyticity, and the *a priori*, discussed above.[24] The idea is, however, that since "Cicero=Tully" is not knowable *a priori*, nor is it analytic (composed of synonyms, or true in virtue of meaning alone), it was thought that to claim it to be necessary could not be right. But as we will see, Kripke applies his comments on the issue of identity statements made with names or descriptions, and their semantic character, to the deft analysis of the issue of theoretical identities. We turn to his argument next.

Theoretical Identities

The core of Kripke's position on mind-body identity statements lies in the distinction between identity statements composed of rigid designators and those composed with non-rigid designators. The argument begins with the claim that there do exist contingent identities, and that these are meant to be support for the view that mind-body identity is just one more legitimate contingent theoretical identity. The idea is this (1980: 98-99):

> [W]e've found out that light is a stream of photons, but of course it might not have been a stream of photons. Heat is in fact the motion of molecules; we found that out, but heat might not have been the motion of molecules....It's no surprise, therefore, that it can be true as a matter of contingent fact and not of any necessity that feeling pain, or seeing red, is just a certain state of the human body. Such psychophysical identifications can be contingent facts just as the other identities are contingent facts.

To argue to the contrary, Kripke begins by building into his discussion the position he has taken on necessary *a posteriori* truths, such as "water is H$_2$0" and "gold is the substance with atomic number 79." As we saw above, in the section on Twin Earth and semantic externalism, these sorts of theoretical identities were analyzed by Kripke to be necessary, even though they are empirically discovered, and not composed of synonyms. And this is because the term 'water' and the term 'gold,' among others, are rigid designators: they refer to the same substance (whose reference might well be fixed by a description) in every possible world. An identity statement between rigid designators will be necessarily true, if true, because of the nature of rigid reference.

Now, what Kripke will claim is that

pain = c-fiber stimulation

is composed of rigid designators, so that it will have to be necessarily true, if it is true at all. The same goes for the following

heat = the motion of molecules.

Now in order to argue that 'pain=c-fiber stimulation' is *not* necessarily true (and therefore false), Kripke will show that there is a difference between how we fix the reference of an expression like 'heat' or 'light' and how we fix the reference of one like 'pain.'

The argument begins with Kripke's claim that 'heat' is to be understood as a term that refers to a certain phenomenon in the world, and not an internal sensation state. The way he analyzes it is to say that the reference of the term 'heat' is fixed by what is in fact a *contingent* property of the external phenomenon. The external phenomenon happens to cause a certain sensation in us. We fix the reference of 'heat' by citing that sensation, which is contingently a product of the motion of molecules. There is a possible world, after all, with molecules moving around but no people or other conscious beings to *feel* any sensation as produced from that motion; so, though no one *feels* heat, there is still heat (the motion of molecules).

So, Kripke argues, the motion of molecules *happens* to produce a certain sensation in us, and we use that contingent property of the motion of molecules to fix the reference of the term 'heat.' The term 'heat' doesn't *mean* 'the motion of molecules,' and we do not know the identification of heat with the motion of molecules *a priori*; we discover that the phenomenon that happens to cause a certain sensation in us is the motion of molecules.

But once we fix the reference of the term 'heat' by this (contingent) property of the motion of molecules (that they can cause us to feel a sensation), we thereby create a rigid designator. 'Heat' is now a term that picks out *the motion of molecules* in every possible world, because it is *that* physical phenomenon that we have (empirically) discovered causes us to feel the sensation of heat. So 'heat is the motion of molecules,' on Kripke's analysis, is necessarily true, but known *a posteriori*.

Now, Kripke's point is that there is no such move available for the term 'pain' and the identification of pain with a physical state, as the materialist would have it. The difference between the theoretical identification of heat with the motion of molecules and pain with (say) brain state S, is that there is, according to Kripke, a property *of* heat — that it causes us to feel a sensation — that can be used to fix the reference of heat in every possible world; to pick out, that is, the phenomenon that causes us to feel that sensation. But there is no such property of *pain*. Pain itself is *not* an external phenomenon that happens to cause a sensation in us, by which we can fix the reference of the term 'pain.' What Kripke claims is that (1980:151):

> In the case of molecular motion and heat there is something, namely the sensation of heat, which is an intermediary between the external phenomenon and the observer. In the mental-physical case no such intermediary is possible, since here the physical phenomenon is supposed to be identical with the internal phenomenon itself.

As Kripke sees it, that is, there is no accidental property of the reference of 'pain' that can act as the reference-fixing property for the term 'pain.' What pain is, he claims, is picked out by the *property of being pain*, and the property of being pain is going to be simply *what feels like pain*. There is no distinction *pain/what feels like pain* that we can appeal to the way we can for *heat/what feels like heat*. When we use 'what feels like heat' to pick out a phenomenon, we are using a contingent property *of that* phenomenon to settle the reference of the term 'heat.'

But, Kripke argues, we can't do this for 'pain.' In the case of the identity 'heat = the motion of molecules,' what we reveal on analysis is a relation between *three* things that has to be kept precise. There is heat, there is the motion of molecules, and there is *what feels like heat*. Now, heat *is* the motion of molecules, but it didn't have to *feel like heat*. It only contingently *feels like* anything to us; but we use that contingent property of heat to (rigidly) fix the reference of the term 'heat.' So there is an *epistemological* element, so to speak, in how we fix the reference of the term 'heat,' but one that is in effect irrelevant with respect to the metaphysics of the situation. Heat just is the motion of molecules; this is a metaphysical identity that we discover, epistemologically, by way of the contingent fact that the motion of molecules cause us to *feel a sensation* that we call 'heat.'

As Kripke wants to make clear, however, the fact that we fix the reference of the term 'heat' by way of a contingent property of the motion of molecules does not affect the status of the identity statement 'heat = molecular motion.' Both 'heat' and 'molecular motion' are rigid designators, which means that the terms pick out the same thing in every possible world. The point is that both terms pick out one and the same thing in every possible world. So the identity statement is not contingent; it is necessarily true.

Now, we can indeed use the description 'what feels like pain' to fix the reference of 'pain,' but in doing so we are not fixing the reference of the term by way of an accidental property of pain — what *feels like pain* just *is* pain; it's an essential property of pain. It is not available to us is to say that pain is necessarily identical with (say) a physical state *P*, but that we find this out by way of a property that physical state *P* might not have had — such as, for instance, that it *feels like pain*. Whatever feels like pain simply *is* pain. If a state is *epistemically* distinguished from pain, it will be *metaphysically* distinguished from pain. There is nothing that *feels like pain* that isn't *pain*.

Kripke's argument is that *if* "pain=c-fiber stimulation" were a theoretical identity like 'heat = the motion of molecules,' as the view he is denying will claim, then it will be composed of rigid designators, and any identity statement that is composed of rigid designators *and* true will be *necessarily* true. Now, 'pain' is, according to Kripke, a rigid designator (and so is 'c-fiber stimulation'). But according to Kripke (as we have spelled out), what the term 'pain' refers to is picked out by an *essential* property of what pain is; and not some contingent property of a physical object. In other words, there is no theoretical discovery that takes us from *what feels like pain* to (say) some brain state *S* with the contingent property of *causing us to feel pain*. What we refer to when we use the rigid designator 'pain' in all possible worlds is *pain itself;* which is what *feels like pain* — and nothing else. What feels like pain thus could very well exist without anything else; there is no reason to suppose that it *is* anything other than what it is — that is, a sensation state. By contrast, the rigid designator 'heat' takes us, by way of a contingent property *of* the phenomenon of heat (what it feels like), to the phenomenon itself — the motion of molecules.

The upshot of Kripke's argument, thus, is twofold: first, that genuine theoretical identities will be necessarily true even if they are discovered to (be so) *a posteriori*; and second, that the purported identity statement 'pain = brain state *S*' is not a true theoretical identity. The reference of the term 'pain' is pain itself, which is not (for instance) a contingent property of something like a physical state. So it is quite possible for a pain to be a pain (a conscious state) and not another thing (a physical state, say). So it can't be *necessarily* true that pain is c-fiber stimulation (or some other physical state). But if it's not necessarily true, it isn't true at all, on Kripke's view.

Essential Properties and the Necessity of Origin

Kripke's discussion of identity statements in Lecture III is best understood by way of what could be the most influential element of his work, the distinction between epistemological properties and metaphysical properties. As we have seen, Lecture III of *Naming and Necessity* builds a picture that comprises Kripke's position on the necessary *a posteriori*, but also includes, more explicitly, a discussion that centers around the issue of essential properties: the necessity of origin. This is an issue that has seen its share of controversy, and we will conclude our discussion of *Naming and Necessity* by drawing together Kripke's well-known claims about the necessity of origin with those of the epistemological and metaphysical status of identity statements.

What lies behind this argument is also relevant to the status of identity statements between referring expressions, which Kripke has defended must be necessarily true if true at all, if composed of rigid designators, in opposition to a long historical view about the role of names and descriptions in identity statements (as we saw above). The context of the argument is that there are indeed properties — being born of one's very parents, for instance — such that one could not shed them and remain metaphysically identical (the *same* person). Reference to a particular individual by a proper name respects these properties (these essential properties) if we recognize that reference to a particular individual is effected by rigid designators. Even if the reference of a rigid designator is *fixed* by describing a *contingent* property of the particular in question, rigid designators are not descriptive in content — they are stipulated to refer to *that* very particular in *every* possible world.

Now, earlier in this chapter, I claimed that there is an analogy we can draw with respect to the case of particulars referred to by names and natural kinds referred to by general nouns ('water,' 'tiger,' 'gold'). In fixing the reference of natural kind terms it is natural to appeal to what might be called 'appearance' properties: what the kind *looks like* or appears to be like perceptually. But as we saw above, what Kripke and Putnam claimed was that the object of reference of a natural kind term is not what it appears to be, but, rather, what it is *essentially*. The appearance properties are contingent properties of the kind, and referring by means of them could deliver quite another thing in another possible world. Appearance properties are descriptive in content, in the pejorative sense.

So the reference of natural kind terms must appeal to what the substance in question really *is*; and this, Kripke argues, is a question of discovery, in empirical cases like the reference of 'water,' 'tiger,' or 'gold.' That it is *discovered*, however, that water is H_2O, and that we cannot hold that 'water' and 'H_2O' are synonyms, does not entail that the discovered identity is not necessarily true. Kripke then adapts the intuition about the necessary *a priori* to the case of other theoretical identities, and shows to resounding effect that mind-body identity — so-called — cannot be analyzed the same way as genuine theoretical identities.

Kripke makes this argument plausible by asking, along the way, what our intuitions regarding the necessity of origin are (1980: 110-12). These claims are meant to provide support for the view that essential properties are not ill-conceived, which, in turn, provides further support for Kripke's claim that that referring to an individual particular with a name is to do so rigidly. Rigid designation, of course, underscores the view that idea that identity is not based on synonymy; that necessity can be discovered *a posteriori,* and that theoretical identities, if true, are necessarily true.

Using a modal supposition, Kripke argues for the plausibility of at least one essential property — that of one's own origin. Kripke argues that it *can't* be that *this very lectern* could have been made of ice, say, or that *the very woman who is presently Queen of England* could have been the daughter of Mr. and Mrs. Truman. There are many properties that the lectern and the Queen presently have that they might not have had: the lectern could have not been in the room that day; the Queen might not have become Queen (her uncle might never have abdicated); but as Kripke puts it (1980: 113):

> One is given, let's say, a previous history of the world up to a certain time, and from that time it diverges considerably from the actual course. This seems to be possible. And so it's possible that even though she was born of these parents she

never became queen. What is harder to imagine is her being born of different parents. It seems to me that anything coming from a different origin would not be this object.

Now, as we have seen, according to Kripke, to make identity statements by way of rigid designators is to make a statement about the way the world is. And one of the ways the world is is that things are necessarily identical with themselves. To say that *x* could be otherwise, as Kripke analyzes it, is not to say *this x could be not x* (Aristotle might not have been Aristotle, say).[25] It is, rather, to make the claim that *of this x*, that the following is the case: it might have been *y*. For instance *of this woman*, that the following might not have been the case: she might not have had the property of being Queen of England.[26]

This way of putting it allows us to refer to a particular object and to continue to do so when we ask what could have been the case regarding *it*. And it was this that we alluded to at the beginning of the chapter as the motivating intuition behind Kripke's analysis of the content of names and other referring expressions. What we have seen here is the development of the concept of rigid designation through that of essentialism, illustrated by way of examples defending the necessity of origin; its adaptation to the topic of theoretical identities (and their metaphysical and epistemological status), and, finally, its role in Kripke's ultimate denial of mind-body identity.

Conclusion

Kripke's views in *Naming and Necessity* have had a profound effect on philosophy. For many of those of the post-Kripke generation, the issues that Kripke argues for and defends seem practically obvious by now. Names are rigid designators; 'water is H_2O' is a necessary truth; identity is not synonymy; it is confused to believe that what is necessary must also be *a priori*; *this* lectern *could not have* been made of ice — these theses have been absorbed and adapted by a whole generation of philosophers who, to some extent, cannot quite grasp how anyone could have thought otherwise. Here I have tried to show the impact of Kripke's views on the history of analytic philosophy by critically analyzing the arguments behind his position.

It is difficult to point to one single work that stands as Kripke's own greatest achievement — so much of his work is and remains influential. It is safe to say, however, that among the greatest achievements of 20th century philosophy are the three short lectures known as *Naming and Necessity*.

ENDNOTES

[1] We discuss these below.

[2] Whitehead and Russell 1910-13.

[3] Frege (1980).

[4] Frege (1980).

[5] Russell (1919).

[6] Russell (1919).

[7] One puzzle, notably discussed by Kripke in his paper "A Puzzle About Belief," (Kripke 1979) is, briefly, as follows. There are, apparently, some contexts of discourse that lead to violation of what is known as the law of substitutivity: the principle that, if two terms have the same reference, they should be replaceable, one for the other, in a sentence, without causing any change in the truth-value of that sentence. Hence, if 'Thomas Mopather' refers to a certain man, and 'Tom Cruise' refers to the *same* man, then "Tom Cruise starred in *Top Gun,*' if true, should remain true when 'Thomas Mopather" replaces 'Tom Cruise' in the sentence.

Contexts of discourse such as belief-contexts, however, appear to be counterexamples to the law of substitutivity. I can believe that Tom Cruise starred in *Top Gun* without believing that Thomas Mopather starred in *Top Gun.* In short, belief-contexts have untoward consequences for a theory of meaning that claims that the meaning of an expression is what it refers to. Kripke shows that contexts involving translation from one language to another have the same untoward effects, highlighting the problem from another angle.

[8] I should say here that in what follows I am concerned to set out Kripke's position as clearly as possible; where appropriate, however, I will highlight disputes.

[9] Marcus (1993). In fact, the topic of combining quantification with modality, with tangents toward essentialism, was the subject of a philosophical discussion between Quine and Marcus in 1962, at which Kripke was present. It has (eyebrow-raisingly) been recently claimed that during this discussion, Kripke heard Marcus make philosophical points that he later appropriated as his own in *Naming and Necessity.* For both the original claim and an uncompromising rebuttal to the charge of misappropriation, see Fetzer and Humphreys (2000). See also Holt (1995) and

Neale (2001) for overview and commentary on the issue.

[10] It is safe to say that *Naming and Necessity* is so thick with genuinely profound philosophical points, that it is a slight disservice to the text, and the way it reads, to have to tease them free from their background; it seems artificial. There aren't too many other options, however.

[11] See Preti (1992, 1995) for development of this position.

[12] Putnam (1973).

[13] What I call semantic externalism has been distinguished as *strong* and *weak* externalism (McGinn 1989), and otherwise emerges in the literature in various guises. Among these are: anti-individualism; the failure of the supervenience of the mental on internal states; wide content; broad content; and the theory of direct reference. See Burge (1979), Fodor (1987), and McGinn (1989).

[14] See Burge (1979; 1986); McGinn (1989).

[15] More on the cluster concept theory below.

[16] See Preti (2000).

[17] On the latter, see Preti (1995).

[18] Kripke (1980:74).

[19] In fact, as Kripke cites, Searle (1958) claims that 'it is a necessary fact that Aristotle has the logical sum, inclusive disjunction, of properties commonly attributed to him.' (Kripke 1980: 74).

[20] Cf. Dummett (1972).

[21] See Burge (1979).

[22] Frege (1879).

[23] Smart (1959).

[24] See Preti (1992;1995) for further elaboration.

[25] Kripke (1980: 62), fn. 25.

[26] But note what Kripke says about assimilating this issue to one concerning scope distinctions (1980: 62):

> Most of the things commonly attributed to Aristotle are things that Aristotle might not have done at all. In a situation in which he didn't do them, we would describe that as a situation in which *Aristotle* didn't do them. This is not a distinction of scope, as happens sometimes in the case of descriptions, where someone might say that the man who taught Alexander might not have taught Alexander; though it could not have been true that: the man who taught Alexander didn't teach

Alexander....Not only is it true *of* the man Aristotle that he might not have gone into pedagogy; it is also true that we use the term 'Aristotle' in such a way that, in thinking of a counterfactual situation in which Aristotle didn't go into any of the fields...commonly attributed to him, still we would say that was a situation in which *Aristotle* did not do these things.

3

On Rules and Private Language: Kripke on Wittgenstein

Introduction

In 1982, Kripke published *Wittgenstein: On Rules and Private Language*, joining a large list of commentators on the work of Ludwig Wittgenstein (1889-1951), one of the 20th century's most extraordinary philosophers.[1] Kripke's book generated more than a little attention and controversy, based on the interpretation he made of some of the most notoriously difficult passages of Wittgenstein's posthumously published *Philosophical Investigations* (1953).[2]

Wittgenstein exegesis is notoriously fraught with difficulty. Examining Wittgenstein's views in isolation from a wider picture of his concerns is difficult — his ideas, and, moreover, his approach, are highly original. To add to the challenge here, Kripke's views center on a set of particular issues in Wittgenstein, which are difficult to appreciate out of context. In order to better understand Kripke's interpretation, we will begin with an exposition of the themes[3] in *Philosophical Investigations,* to give some background to Kripke's comments, and then go on to elaborate Kripke's views.

The youngest of eight children of a rich Austrian businessman (three of whom committed suicide), Wittgenstein went to England to study engineering in 1908. During his studies he became interested in the foundations of mathematics, and came across the work of Bertrand Russell on that subject. He abandoned engineering and went to Cambridge in 1911 to study with Russell. From 1911 to 1951, when he died, Wittgenstein's presence in academic philosophy (and his notable absences from it) stands as the most unorthodox and fascinating of any other philosopher of that period. Wittgenstein couldn't stand formal academic life, and seems to have had little patience for the ambiguities of human nature. He is reported to have been (among other things) difficult, eccentric, brash, and exacting (his work exhibiting these traits as well) but he is considered one of the few true geniuses in philosophy.[4]

Wittgenstein published only one book and one article in his entire career as a philosopher. His style of composition was to write copious notes on a topic, distill those that expressed ideas he wished to preserve into still other notes, and, finally, prepare a compressed final draft. Wittgenstein's reputation is partly grounded on a book he did not publish during his lifetime (but that he was working on until he died), now considered one of the key texts of 20th century philosophy. *Philosophical Investigations* (hereafter *PI*) has been pored over by countless philosophers. It is a difficult text, cryptic, terse, and sometimes obscure, and there is little consensus on its correct interpretation.[5] *PI* is sometimes thought to be a repudiation of the philosophical commitments of Wittgenstein's first book, *Tractatus Logico-Philosophicus* (published in 1921), a work that was written, among other things, in order to solve the problems of logic and language that concerned him (and his teacher Russell) in the early part of the century. *Philosophical Investigations* appears to reject the picture of language that *Tractatus* defends, but the themes and topics are similar, even if the approach is not.

Wittgenstein does not seem to have wavered in his belief that language, and understanding language correctly, was the foundation of philosophy, and the key to solving the problems of philosophy. At the core of any philosophical investigation of language are the concepts of meaning and understanding: and these form the key topics around which *Philosophical Investigations* is constructed. *PI* is not, however, a work that is particularly perspicuous. It is not, for instance, written as a series of premises and conclusions meant to defend a theory of language, meaning, or understanding. Rather (Wittgenstein 1958: v):

> I have written down all these thoughts as *remarks*, short paragraphs.....The best that I could write would never be more than philosophical remarks; my thoughts were soon crippled if I tried to force them on in any single direction against their natural inclination. —And this was, of course, connected with the very nature of the investigation. For this compels us to travel over a wide field of thought criss-cross in every direction.

It is worthwhile mentioning this here because, as we will see, Kripke's approach to the elucidation of Wittgenstein's position in certain key passages of *PI* was, among other things, criticized for imposing on Wittgenstein's text something that Wittgenstein seemed by his own lights particularly anxious to avoid. Wittgenstein did not take himself to be offering a theory, but, if anything, a journey through topics that (as he claims) show themselves to be interrelated. Nothing at all is presupposed about the notions of meaning and understanding: the concepts themselves dictate the investigation we should make of them. What this means for Wittgenstein is that we should avoid the temptation to see these concepts as other than they are. And to avoid the temptation we must be encouraged to see what the temptation is.

Wittgenstein takes himself to be offering what calls a *grammatical* investigation of the concepts at the heart of language, something that constitutes part of his unique approach to these issues. The idea is that if we look to the way that the concepts of language, meaning or understanding relate to other concepts (by looking at the way we *use* those concepts, for instance), we may begin to see that to cling to a certain view about meaning and understanding is simply wrong, or, at best, indefensible. For instance (*PI* 90):

> We feel as if we had to *penetrate* phenomena: our investigation, however, is directed not towards phenomena, but, as one might say, towards the *'possibilities'* of phenomena....Our investigation is therefore a grammatical one. Such an investigation sheds light on our problem by clearing misunderstandings away. Misunderstandings concerning the use of words, caused, among other things, by certain analogies between the forms of expression in different regions of language.

This, among others, is a passage where Wittgenstein discusses what a grammatical investigation can accomplish. Chief among its advantages is that it is *descriptive*; a descriptive investigation can deliver, in his view, the clearest view of the concepts of language, meaning and understanding (*PI* 109, 124, 126).

This is because we are, for various reasons, according to Wittgenstein, tempted not just to hold or to cling to a certain conception of meaning and of understanding (and thus also of language), but also to *impose* it — and even to alter what we observe so that it conforms (even just to our satisfaction) to this conception. Wittgenstein takes himself to have been guilty of succumbing to this sort of temptation in his early work. But this conception — tempting as it may be — can be resisted if we simply *look* at the role that language plays in our customs, our practice, and our lives, as well as its role *as* a custom, or a practice, in our lives (*PI* 66).

For Wittgenstein, the best way to achieve clarity in what we see when we investigate language is by describing the way we use language (among other things), shoring this up by countless examples and counterexamples, meant to dislodge the roots of our (mistaken) pre-conceptions of it. It is a testament, perhaps, to the entrenchedness of that preconception that Wittgenstein's attempt to dislodge it should read so opaquely, and be so difficult, and so demanding.

Meaning, Understanding, and Rules

Philosophical Investigations is composed of two parts. Part I is conventionally divided more or less into the following themes. It begins with a criticism of the view of language and meaning that Wittgenstein himself defended in *Tractatus*; includes remarks on the nature and aim of philosophy; shifts to a series of remarks known as the the 'rule-following considerations'; shifts again to what is known as the 'private language argument'; and ends with a series of remarks on the philosophy of psychology, including his thoughts on introspection, imagination, seeing, and consciousness (among others).

Wittgenstein exegesis is staggeringly large.[6] There are, by now, countless commentaries on his work (his executors made his unpublished manuscripts available after his death), journals and conferences devoted to his work, biographies, and memoirs — and ongoing disputes. This is no surprise, of course: the work itself is challenging to think and write about; and the obscurity of the style allows no small scope for disagreement. It is possible, however, that no commentary on the work of Wittgenstein generated the kind of attention and controversy that Saul Kripke's did, when it appeared.

Kripke concentrates mainly on what he believes to be at work in the sections of *PI* concerned with rules and private language, so, in what follows, we will restrict our comments to the remarks Wittgenstein makes on the nature of meaning; the passages on rule-following, and those on private language in *PI*.

Language, Meaning, the Language-Game, and Forms of Life

What are perhaps the most well-known passages in *PI* are those that concern the nature of meaning. One of the few positive statements of Wittgenstein's of the nature of meaning is this (*PI* 43):

For a *large* class of cases — though not for all — in which we employ the word "meaning" it can be defined thus: the meaning of a word is its use in the language.

As commentators[7] have noted, at length, what Wittgenstein appears to be concerned to deny is a conception of meaning understood as an 'inner state' or 'inner process.' Wittgenstein's stalking horse has been variously described as something hidden, mentalistic, and private. What Wittgenstein does appear to want to elucidate, and counter, is the conviction, mistakenly elevated into theory, that meaning is a mental/inner state or process that *accompanies* our use of signs, suspended (somehow) before the mind, and which constitutes their meaning (*PI* 153):

> We are trying to get hold of the mental process of understanding which seems to be hidden behind those coarser and therefore more readily visible accompaniments. But we do not succeed; or, rather, it does not get as far as a real attempt. For even supposing I had found something that happened in all those cases of understanding, —why should *it* be the understanding? And how can the process of understanding have been hidden, when I said "Now I understand" *because* I understood?! And if I say it is hidden—then how do I know what I have to look for? I am in a muddle.

Similarly, in *PI* (154):

> …Try not to think of understanding as a 'mental process' at all.— For *that* is the expression that confuses you. But ask yourself: in what sort of case, in what kind of circumstances, do we say, "Now I know how to go on," when, that is, the formula *has* occurred to me?—

> In the sense in which there are processes (including mental processes) which are characteristic of understanding, understanding is not a mental process.

> (A pain's growing more and less; the hearing of a tune or a sentence: these are mental processes.)

So it appears plausible to say (with all the usual provisos about interpreting Wittgenstein in place) that all in all, the text of *PI* does express the negative claim that Wittgenstein wants to uphold: that meaning is not an isolated and independent state of mind that is (somehow) associated with our expressions, something we intend to convey, and mysteriously project onto the world by way of those expressions. [8]

The conception of language that Wittgenstein instead wants to put across in *PI* takes language to be part of our natural history (*PI* 25), something that is best explained by conceiving it as the use of signs to communicate within a context (loosely, a 'form of life'), and that involves abilities characterized as customs, habits, and practices (*PI* 7, 19). The context(s) of language and the role of language as a means of communication — the activities we call language — is given close attention (the 'language-game' *PI* 7). Much like the concept of a game (*PI* 66, 67, 75), according to Wittgenstein, the concept of language comprises different sorts of things, and to try to give theoretically structured necessary and sufficient conditions for what language is (similarly, for 'game') is taking the wrong tack. The most important thing, philosophically speaking, is to respect the *different* uses of signs, see what resemblance there is between them (*PI* 67), come to be familiar with them, and see them for what they are (*PI* 66), instead of trying to fit them into a model that may or may not be suitable for *some* of the signs of our language (*PI* 3).

Rules and Rule-Following

Now, closely connected to the issue of language and communication is the notion of *correct* use of our signs: *normativity* seems to play a significant role in communication. Presumably we can communicate in the first place because we employ signs that we understand and that others understand. There would appear to be some uniformity to meaning and understanding since we don't have to explain and re-explain ourselves — or reinvent some system of symbolic representation — each time we use signs to communicate. So, what does this uniformity consist of? How does it work? What *is* at bottom of the notion that a sign means *this* but not *that*? What makes it correct to use one sign rather than another? What does that correctness consist of? What *determines* what makes one sign mean one thing rather than another?

These questions, of course, form part of the larger question at the heart of the concept of language, and the one that concerns Kripke, as we will see. The larger question is: what is it that determines the meaning of our signs? What is the *nature* of meaning? As noted above, Wittgenstein took it that whatever the meaning of our signs consists of, it is not an inner state. What Wittgenstein wants to emphasize is the *use* of signs: their application (there in the context of life just the way it is lived); the variety of communicative relations we have in our human life, and what this variety can tell us about language, meaning, and

70

understanding. But the concept of sign-application raises puzzles that need investigation.[9]

PI 138 is the passage that is conventionally taken to introduce a series of remarks known as the 'rule-following considerations.' From *PI* 138 to 242, Wittgenstein investigates the notion of the use of a sign over time; the grasp of a sign and the use we make of it on repeated subsequent occasions (among other things). Wittgenstein sees a puzzle in the understanding or grasp of the meaning of a sign and the *application* of it thereafter (*PI* 139):

> When someone says the word "cube" to me, for example, I know what it means. But can the whole *use* of the word come before my mind, when I *understand* it in this way?

Or, again (*PI* 151):

> ...A writes series of numbers down; B watches him and tries to find a law for the sequence of numbers. If he succeeds he exclaims: "Now I can go on" ——So this capacity, this understanding, is something that makes its appearance in a moment. So let us try and see what it is that makes its appearance here.

What Wittgenstein highlights is that grasping a sign is (somehow) grasping the *application* of the sign. And, in an important move, what Wittgenstein claims is that *application* of a sign involves the notion of *following a rule*.

The capacity to use a sign (to understand a sign) is, according to Wittgenstein, puzzling in that such understanding is not, by nature, a one-time thing. If you truly understand a sign, you understand *how to apply it*, which introduces the notion of sustained future instances of understanding. Moreover, this understanding, and its projection into the future, is bound by issues of correctness. You understand how to apply the sign *the right way*, infinitely many times — that haven't even taken place yet. The concepts of future use, future correct use, future uniform use, and the like, are what Wittgenstein discusses as 'rule-following.' The question, or puzzle, is what determines the understanding and meaning of our signs, given that we use them over and over, the same way. [10]

The rule-following considerations can be read as putting continued pressure on the conviction or temptation to think of meaning or understanding as a mental state, an independent, inner, hidden, and isolated entity that queerly appears before the mind, and whose presence dictates whether or not we 'understand' or grasp the meaning of our signs. So the rule-following considerations can be construed as an example of the revelation that Wittgenstein makes about the nature of language, meaning, and understanding. That is, rules and their nature are naturally connected to the view that meaning is *use*, as Wittgenstein takes his investigation to reveal. We *use* signs to communicate, and we communicate, successfully (correctly) time and time and time again, consistently and productively. Something must govern this ability; the nature of meaning and understanding, to be sure, but now what we (should) see is that this involves the capacity to follow a rule, and to do so correctly. What Wittgenstein seems to emphasize is that such a capacity cannot plausibly be a hidden, inner, mental state or process.

To see this, consider that to use an English word is to (implicitly) follow a set of rules. A natural language has rules of grammar (syntax) and semantic rules (governing what a word means and how it is to be employed). So to *know* English, to *understand* English, is to follow a rule for the application of its signs. Consider that there are infinitely many uses of the word 'subway' you might make for the rest of your life. If you understand English you will do so and do so correctly *every* time. Wittgenstein's query is twofold: just what is the nature of those rules; and, when you learned the word 'subway,' were *all* those rule-governed uses part of grasping its meaning? After all, as we have said, using a sign is not just using *that* sign at *that* time; the use of a sign takes place in the context of communication: different times, places, needs, intentions, etc. And we *do* communicate. We are able to use a finite number of signs infinitely many times and in infinite contexts; think of the 26 letters of the English alphabet, and the infinitely many words and sentences we can produce and understand. What we understand, when we grasp the meaning of a sign, according to Wittgenstein, is *how to go on to use it*. Wittgenstein calls this 'following a rule,' thus expanding his investigation of meaning and understanding to the concept of *normativity*; rightness or correctness.

Normativity: Rules and Private Language

The investigation into the application of a sign thus appears to play an important role in putting pressure on the mentalistic conception of understanding the meaning of a sign, and to unfold and clarify a set of concepts Wittgenstein has found to be interrelated. Remember that the notion of meaning under siege is one that claims that understanding the meaning of a sign is possessing (somehow) an isolable mentalistic entity, like a shadow, associated with the sign, that you intend to convey with your use of the sign. But since understanding the meaning of a sign will involve *application* of it, the question arises as to what it can mean to understand something that essentially involves future and consistent application.

According to Wittgenstein, no isolated and independent mental state could 'contain' or constitute this sort of projectible ability, and thus, no such thing can be the nature of meaning. Note that the notion of pointing to anything like isolated, independent, mental entity to be the constitutive element of 'understanding a rule' is far-fetched, at best. How could an ability be such thing? How is the normativity that constitutes that ability captured in such a thing? If understanding a sign involves following a rule, and the nature of rule-following can't be characterized plausibly as a hidden, inner, mental process, then the chances of the nature of meaning itself being constituted as a hidden and inner mental process are diminished.

So Wittgenstein's investigation of meaning and understanding seems to take the form, in the rule-following considerations, of asking for the basis upon which we ground a criterion for using/applying a sign, given that it has emerged that the nature of *grasping* a sign will involve not just applying it *today* but from now *on*, and, in addition, applying it *correctly* from now on. Wittgenstein is occupied with a puzzle that he sees arising in the gap between the nature of grasping the meaning of a sign and going on to use that sign, on a certain (mistaken) conception of meaning.

This analysis of Wittgenstein's position helps in the task of highlighting more explicitly what Kripke claims to have been struck by in his analysis of Wittgenstein; for Kripke's analysis emphasizes another problematic aspect with respect to the nature of meaning and understanding, namely, what determines meaning to begin with, as we will see.

Now, as we have seen, Wittgenstein's investigation is concerned with the nature of meaning, and he appears to be concerned to deny a mental/inner state or process criterion of meaning. To do this, Wittgenstein appears to marshal a number of points about rules, rule-following, use, application, and the like to make his refutation of that view most effective. But this does raise a question that never did evaporate entirely, namely: what *does* determine the meaning of a sign? If it isn't an inner state, then what it is it? What if it turns out that we cannot find *any* plausible criteria that will determine the nature of meaning, understood as the ability to use/apply a sign? In such a case, not only is the whole concept of following a rule obscured, the whole concept of meaning *anything at all* by any of our signs is called into question.

This is the issue that constitutes the basis of Kripke's analysis of Wittgenstein. Kripke calls it 'the sceptical paradox;' the view, in brief, that there is nothing at all that determines the meaning of our signs. Kripke will claim that in the course of his remarks on the nature of rule-following, Wittgenstein reveals, accepts, and solves the sceptical paradox, and that an analysis of how this is done sheds light, among other things, on Wittgenstein's renowned argument against a private language. We turn to a brief exposition of the private language argument next, in order to set the stage for Kripke's analysis.

The Private Language Argument: PI 243-275

One way to read the private language argument, as the series of remarks 243-275 in *PI* are conventionally known, is as Wittgenstein's attempt to mount a *prima facie* case *for* the mentalistic, inner, private conception of meaning — in order, ultimately, to deny it. *PI* 243-275 can be read as Wittgenstein's meticulous consideration of what appears to be a counterexample to his claim that meaning is not an inner mentalistic entity-like state, and his answer to it.

Kripke, however, claims that there is another angle. The overarching issue here, as we have seen, appears to be the nature of meaning and understanding, and, in particular, what determines the meaning of a sign. What Kripke takes the private language argument to be about is this: if the nature of meaning involves the nature of application of a sign, then what of the signs for our own first-person states? What governs *their* application? Could it just be a set of criteria that involve reference to nothing other than facts about me alone?[11] If so, what does this entail about the concept of meaning, understood as application or use of a sign? Can *I* decide what rules there are, and which rules to follow, in my use of (some of my) signs? And if so, what, if anything, does this entail for the nature of meaning of the signs in a language?

Kripke takes the sceptical paradox to be at the heart of Wittgenstein's investigation, and he reads the private language argument as providing the ingredients for what he calls the 'sceptical solution' to it. Kripke tackles Wittgenstein's text from the point of view of the outcome that a putative form of sensation (private)-language might have for the sceptical paradox. A private language, that is, seems to have what it takes to thwart the sceptical paradox, since it seems to be precisely the sort of use of a sign that *does* have a definitive criterion. That is, the meaning of my sensation words could (if *anything* could) seem to be plausibly established by *my* private, inner, mental, and hidden decisions and intentions with respect to what my sensation-words mean. But what Kripke wants to show is that Wittgenstein denies this, by (allegedly) repudiating the 'private' aspect of a private language.

Now, a significant element of Wittgenstein's position is the attempt to deny an inner process or inner state criterion of meaning. Kripke does not see the text this way — at least, he doesn't write about it that way. We should, however, comment on this angle, before going on to elaborate Kripke's position, to lay the foundation for a summary of these issues, at the conclusion of this chapter.

On the face of it, there does seem to be one set of concepts for which the criteria for application appear to be restricted to facts about *me*: the first-person concepts that I use to refer to my sensation-states, like pain. If anything seems to be hidden, inner, mentalistic, or even to possess entity-like borders, my sensation states seem to. To consider the concept of 'pain,' or to be asked to visualize 'pain,' does seem to call up some sort of mental entity — an *experience* —before the mind, so it appears to make sense to say that the *meaning* of our sensation-words are determined by hidden, private, inner mental states or processes.

The topic of sensation-states and how we refer to them thus seems to be the opportunity Wittgenstein takes to ask: could the semantic character of an entire language — the words for sensations states and everything else — plausibly be constructed along the model that seems to make sense for signs for our sensation-states?

The answer, according to Wittgenstein, is no. What Wittgenstein attempts to do in the private language argument is deny that *even* words for sensation-states could have their meaning determined by an inner state or process. What Wittgenstein brings to bear are his remarks about the nature of meaning and understanding (which include the notion following a rule), against the topic of the meaning of sensation-signs, a plausible candidate for the inner state conception of meaning.

What Wittgenstein contends is that we can no more restrict the meaning of our sensation-words to a private inner mental and hidden realm than we can for any other of the words in our language. Sensation-words are *part of language*; and language, and meaning, for Wittgenstein, turns on use, application, and, most important, *correct* application, in the context of communication (*PI* 258). The concept of application of a sign introduces the concept of rule-following, which itself embeds a concept of normativity. To follow a rule is to get something *right*. Normativity is one way of highlighting the big picture — to ask what is it that determines the nature of meaning will be to ask what makes it correct to apply *this* sign; *this* sign rather than another; and what makes it possible to say 'now I can go on' (*PI* 151).

The link between Wittgenstein's consideration of the private language argument and rule-following appears to rest on the central importance of the concept of normativity in his investigation of the nature of meaning. Wittgenstein appears to show in the passages that contain the private language argument that (if it is coherent at all) a private language is, in fact, a reductio: you yourself wouldn't understand it (*PI* 257). Why is this? Because *appearing to understand* and *understanding* collapse into each other on the conception of private meaning and understanding. Normativity, therefore, is sacrificed in a private language — but this is a non-negotiable element of meaning and understanding, which embed the notion of following a rule. There couldn't *be* a genuine language whose conditions of application did not include an account of normativity — and a so-called private language is precisely one that doesn't. So, Wittgenstein concludes, the concept of a private language is one that cannot be defended, at best; incoherent, at worst.

Now, Kripke's reading of Wittgenstein will involve thinking of the private language argument as a special case of what he calls the 'sceptical paradox,' which, Kripke argues, is, ultimately, to be found in the passages on rule-following in *PI*. In fact, as Kripke claims, the *real* private language argument is to be found long before the passages that are traditionally believed to contain it (*PI* 243-275). Kripke's reading of Wittgenstein, and his attribution of what he calls a sceptical paradox, and sceptical solution to Wittgenstein, definitively influenced the course of Wittgenstein scholarship and exegesis as of the appearance his book in 1982 — no small feat, considering that, even then, the number of pages devoted to Wittgenstein analysis and commentary were overwhelmingly many. The publication of Kripke's book saw what could be called a cottage industry arise on the subject of rule-following and private language, one that shows little sign of abating, almost 20 years later. We turn to Kripke's arguments next.

The Sceptical Paradox

In the Introductory section to *Wittgenstein: On Rules and Private Language* (Kripke 1982) Kripke writes that his interpretation[12] of Wittgenstein is to be understood as (1982: 5):

> [t]he set of problems and arguments which I personally have gotten out of reading Wittgenstein...the present paper should be thought of as expounding neither 'Wittgenstein's' argument nor 'Kripke's': rather Wittgenstein's argument as it struck Kripke, as it presented a problem for him.

Kripke begins by claiming that, on his interpretation, the 'private language argument' is "principally to be explicated in terms of the problem of 'following a rule'" (1982: vi), and starts by considering the example of understanding the 'meaning' of the sign '+.' If we consider what it is to understand this sign, we might consider the various ways in which we learned the context and function of that sort of sign— probably by example. We have been shown pairs of integers, for instance, and been told and/or shown by example that when '+' features in between pairs, this signals a relation that is to occur between them. The relation is called 'addition': the presence of '+' between two integers is meant to have a *result,* namely, the sum of the two quantities referred to by the terms flanking the sign.

We would say that someone demonstrates understanding of '+' under conditions where she produces what we would call the 'right' answer time after time. So the question is: what determines that understanding? Kripke puts it like this: to *understand* addition is to *grasp a rule,* in that to grasp a rule is to have past *intentions* that determine a particular answer, and the same one, in the presence of '+,' every time.

A "bizarre"[13] sceptic, however, raises the following doubt: how does my present ability with respect to addition determine what I intended by 'addition' in the *past*? What does giving the answer '125' to the question "what is '68+57?'" demonstrate (if anything) about what, and in virtue of what, that answer is generated? To put it another way (epistemologically): How can what I do now give a justification for my using the rule for addition when I do? [14]

After all, says the sceptic, what can we really say to refute the contention that maybe in the past I meant something *else* by 'addition'? Who's to say that maybe, in the past, what I meant by 'addition' was that for '68 + 57' to add up to '125,' whatever takes the second argument place in the function had to be less than 57. If it was more, then '68+ (*n* > 57)' will equal 5. Kripke calls *this* function 'quaddition,' and the sceptical paradox is off and running. The issue is: what makes me think I didn't *always* mean 'quus' by 'plus'? The sceptic's point is that *nothing* in my giving the answer '125' this time in fact rules out *another* answer.

To see this, we can focus on the essence of Kripke's example here. 'Quus' is defined in such a way that my *present* performance with respect to '68+57' could conform *either* to 'quus,' or to 'plus': the idea is that 'quus' is a function that holds of numbers in the second argument place that are *less than* 57. If we stipulate for the sake of the example that this is the first time I have added two numbers, one of which was 57, then I am in conformity with the 'quus' computational rules — but also with those of 'plus.' The sceptical problem is: is there anything about what I would call my understanding of 'plus' that could decide the issue as to which function I meant; and, therefore, which answer is *correct*?

Now, it seems that the initial answer to the sceptic would be disbelief. At first blush we seem to know and be able to defend quite well what we mean an arithmetical function like addition. But on sober analysis, the issue turns on just what 'grasping the rule' consists of. Our initial intuition is to say that when I go to compute a sum I've never come across before, I confidently apply a rule I have already learned, knowing what it means. But, as Kripke claims, by way of the sceptic, this raises the deeper issue of *what it is to mean* 'addition' instead of 'quaddition' or, from the epistemological perspective, *what it is that justifies me* in claiming that the answer to '68+57' is 125, and *not* 5; that is, what makes me so sure that there is a *right* answer to this problem? And what, from the metaphysical perspective, is the nature of *a right answer* in a case like this?

What Kripke does in his analysis of a particular rule-following consideration — what our grasping the rule or following the rule for addition consists of — is to highlight what he calls Wittgenstein's recognition of a profound and wholly original philosophical problem of scepticism, represented by a sceptic's comments. What can it mean to say that I am following a rule? What does this consist of? These questions become particularly pressing once we realize that the sceptic's question is, in fact, directed to my taking it for granted that I know what *I* mean by a word in my language. The sceptic's remarks prepare the ground for what Kripke calls the Wittgensteinian or sceptical paradox (1982: 55):

> There can be no such thing as meaning anything by a word. Each new application we make is a leap in the dark; any present intention could be interpreted so as to accord with anything we may choose to do.

The problem arises in part, as Kripke notes, because the concept of rule-following does appear to carry with it the implicit idea that when we apply a rule we do not do so *blindly*. This is intuitively explained by saying that we *have something in mind* when we apply a rule — something we *intend* to do, to follow, to perform, and the like — and that something is what constitutes our grasp or understanding of the rule. Now, as will become clear as we go on, Kripke does not take as his focus the Wittgensteinian arguments against the inner process or inner state theory of meaning, which we suggested above were the object of Wittgenstein's remarks in the rule-following considerations. Rather, Kripke takes the tack of highlighting the connection between the rule-following considerations and those on the subject of a private language — by way of an emphasis derived by a certain reading of 'private,' as we alluded to above.[15]

As Kripke reads Wittgenstein, what is under scrutiny is the issue of determining what I mean by the words I use — whether there is *anything at all* that *can* determine what I mean by the words I use. Kripke construes the problem, that is, as a sceptical issue regarding the determination of meaning from the perspective of a particular speaker, an isolated, independent individual. So we could say that Kripke construes Wittgenstein's negative thesis concerning the nature of meaning as a hidden, inner, mental entity view as one that turns on what an *individual* can accomplish *by herself* in determining meaning.

We can see this by considering what it is that I purportedly have at my disposal against the sceptic; and what it is, Kripke argues, is paper-thin. When asked what makes me think I didn't always mean 'quus' by 'plus,' either in the past, or now in my present use of it, I answer that I *intended* to use '+' in such and such a way; or, I *had in mind* that '+' means such and such, and that this is because I *grasp the rule* for *addition,* and that rule is not the rule for *quaddition.* What the sceptic claims, however, is that nothing in my 'intending' nor in my 'having in mind' can determine *which* of those two very different concepts I take myself to grasp.

After all, what does this grasp I allude to consist in? Did I perform some sort of ceremony, asserting 'what I mean is *'plus''*? Do I perform that meaning-conferring ceremony every time? If so, what is that ceremony? What does it consist of? And how, in particular, does it cover every future computation I might be faced with? Did I perform it *this* time? If not, how can I be so sure that I didn't mean *quus* by 'plus' up to now? What's the difference between a 'quus' conferring meaning-ceremony and a 'plus' conferring one? What do I have to go on to claim that there is a difference? What is there about my understanding of 'plus' that makes *this* computation of 68+57 one more plain old instance of 'addition' and not my first experience with an instance of 'quaddition'? The situation, as Kripke argues, is dire — because, as the sceptic blithely points out, there is nothing I can point to, no fact of the matter, that is not equally determining of 'quus' as it is for 'plus.' It appears that *I* myself don't and can't know what I mean by my own words.

As Kripke reads Wittgenstein, this is the problem at the heart of

On Rules and Private Language

PI — there is nothing at all that can determine what we mean by our signs, and he cites *PI* 201 by way of confirmation of his view:

> This was our paradox: no course of action could be determined by a rule, because every course of action can be made out to accord with a rule […].

That is, as Kripke sees the issue, the sceptical paradox is that meaning and understanding, meaning and intending, and the like, will make no sense.(Kripke 1982:13):

> For the sceptic holds that no fact about my past history — nothing that was ever in my mind, or in my external behavior — establishes that I meant plus rather than quus....

What the sceptical paradox shows, according to Kripke, is that whatever I might claim as a criterion for meaning one thing rather than another collapses under closer scrutiny. I think I know what (say) 'cat' means. But — the sceptic retorts — when I say "Luke is a cat" what makes me so sure what I mean by 'cat'? What can I point to that rules out that what I actually mean is 'dat,' where 'dat' means 'hungry cat if before noon, sleeping cat after noon'? What rules out that instead of 'cat' I've *always* meant 'dat'?[16] According to the sceptic: nothing. It's a free for all. Nothing in my past use of a word determines what I presently mean by it. None of our words mean anything, precisely because they could mean *anything*.

Now, in order to bring out the sceptic's point and to make it most pressing, Kripke assesses three criteria that could, if anything, provide a determination of meaning. Kripke takes these as exhaustive,[17] denies that any of them supply the fact of the matter, and concludes that the sceptical paradox stands; and stands in need of solution. It is Kripke's interpretation of Wittgenstein's solution to the sceptical paradox that is, arguably, what generated the most controversy, as we will see in what follows.

Dispositions

What Kripke identifies as possible candidates for understanding or meaning are: the actual use or application of a sign; states of consciousness that are introspectively accessible and qualitative (an experience, for instance); or a disposition to apply the sign. The first two get fairly short shrift. Actual application cannot ground the putative fact of the matter about what I mean or understand, since alternative meanings are completely consistent with any use or application of the word so far in my linguistic history (see, as above, *quus,* or *dat*). Qualitative states of consciousness, are in effect, no less open to ambiguity, since, even if they are available, they can be variously interpreted and applied. What Kripke puts to a more detailed analysis is the idea that a disposition might supply a genuinely constitutive condition for the nature of meaning and understanding.[18]

A disposition to act can be formulated as what I *would* do in a given situation. Dispositions are auditioned as potentially suitable candidates for *what it is that I mean by 'plus'* (and an answer to the sceptic) because we can (allegedly) say that the fact of the matter in question is what I *would have said* in the past had I been posed the question '68+57'?[19]

Kripke rejects this answer, however, on two grounds. First, he notes, dispositions are *finite*, in effect, no less finite than any performances I executed in the past with the sign '+' or any of the times I used 'cat'. So regarding the issue dispositionally does not advance us past the sceptic, who can continue to reply that there just is no fact of the matter as to what I would say under condition C based on any consideration of what I would have said *had I* been subject to condition C in the past. Second, as Kripke notes, dispositions are *fallible*. We can be disposed to make mistakes, which more or less *strengthens* the sceptic's case. Given the fallible nature of dispositions, isn't it just obvious that whether *what I would have said under condition C* might well be a *mistake*? And if so, that disposition could not constitute what I mean by my words – it would, at best, constitute what I am making *a mistake about* with my words – just the wrong sort of thing to ground meaning one thing rather than another. The sceptical problem, in short, remains firmly in place.

The Sceptical Solution: Assertibility and the Community

The great sceptic in the history of philosophy is invariably thought to be David Hume (1711-1776), and Kripke makes allusions to Hume in what he gleans from Wittgenstein.[20] Kripke suggests we can read Wittgenstein as claiming that there is nothing that constitutes meaning something by a particular word, analogous to Hume's position on causation. Hume argued that we were conditioned, by custom and habit, to infer a necessary causal connection between events A and B, when these events were presented to experience as constantly conjoined and contiguous (as he put it). No idea, however, could be in the mind without an impression preceding it; for Hume, an empiricist, all mental content came from sense-experience. We do not *experience* causation, so our concept of causation arises more from our desires than it does from the world.

Meaning, Kripke suggests, has something of these hallmarks for Wittgenstein. As Kripke reads him, Wittgenstein raises and concedes the sceptical paradox; but takes the burden to be to solve it. It defies intuition, let alone common sense, that we don't mean anything by our words, and that a profound ambiguity reigns over our efforts to communicate through our language. The solution Wittgenstein offers, according to Kripke, ties together the rule-following considerations and the private language argument.

What Kripke argues (on his reading of Wittgenstein) is that the rule-following considerations are a way of formulating the private language argument, by introducing a paradox about what *my grounds are* for claiming that I do and can mean something by my words and what *constitutes* my meaning something by my words. Kripke frames the paradox by way of the rule-following considerations, which, as we argued above, introduce the notion that to mean or to understand a word is to apply it correctly on future occasions. But what Kripke sees in Wittgenstein's argument is not an emphasis on the inner state model of meaning, and a concern to deny this. Rather, what Kripke takes himself to reconstruct from Wittgenstein's text is a defense of the notion of meaning that is erected on the idea that no single individual *can* mean anything by her words.

Now, we argued above that one reading of the private language argument is that of an attempt by Wittgenstein to show that even what looks like a genuinely private language — comprising the words we have for our sensation-states — fails a criterial test for meaning. Nothing can be meaning, nor be graspable by the understanding, unless it carries a normative component. Meaning or understanding is an ability, as Wittgenstein appears to claim, and an ability, if successful, is governed by rules. If the language for our sensation states really were private, Wittgenstein claims, whatever we thought was the correct application of a word *would be*; and the notion of correct application of a word would collapse — a private language sidesteps normativity. As we alluded to above, Wittgenstein uses the example of the words for our sensation states to show that meaning cannot be an inner state or process, even for those words which appear to refer to inner states or processes, because meaning and application go hand in hand. And, for Wittgenstein, the concept of application is one that carries an objectively normative component — something cannot *be* a correct application simply by *seeming* like one.

Now, what Kripke does is take another element as the object of attention in Wittgenstein's position.[21] Kripke draws the line between the rule-following considerations and the private language argument this way: if we can decide privately what the word 'pain' means, which is to decide privately what counts as correct application of it, the word 'pain' could apply to everything, or nothing — such a view would result in there being no such thing as meaning anything by the word 'pain.' This is, of course, the sceptical paradox, which Kripke claims is contained in *PI* 202:

> And hence also 'obeying a rule' is a practice. And to *think* one is obeying a rule is not to obey a rule. Hence it is not possible to obey a rule 'privately,': otherwise thinking one was obeying a rule would be the same thing as obeying it.

And the solution to the paradox, as Kripke claims on his reading of Wittgenstein, is those with whom we communicate.

Kripke reads Wittgenstein's references to 'language and the activities into which it is woven' ('form of life') and the 'language game' to support his contention that it is the community, and not an isolated individual, in a private ceremony, that establishes the nature of meaning. To support this, Kripke argues that we must read Wittgenstein as wanting to repudiate a thesis about meaning based on *truth-conditions* — the view he defended in his early philosophical treatise on logical form and meaning. And Wittgenstein does appear to take a Fregean and Russellian theory of meaning seriously in *Tractatus Logico-Philosophicus*. Frege's theory (see Chapter 2) does appear to claim that meaning is that which points or leads the way to *what makes the sentence true*. Russell's version would be to say that every word in the language corresponds either to a certain kind of particular or to a universal, such that it can make a contribution in a definitive way to the truth or falsity of a sentence.

In *PI*, however Wittgenstein is, by his own lights, clearly dedicated to denying a certain picture of meaning. I argued above that it was an inner mental state or process theory of meaning, one that can be seen to undergird both a Fregean and Russellian theory of meaning,[22] which Wittgenstein criticizes as examples of having succumbed to the temptation to see meaning as an entity that we crystallize in the mind and 'associate' somehow, with our words.

What Kripke claims, however, is that Wittgenstein instead wants to contrast *truth-conditions* with *assertibility-conditions*, by way of his points about the impossibility of obeying a rule 'privately.' The solution to the sceptical paradox is not that there is *something* expressed by our words, which counts as their meaning, which we understand, associate with our words, and entertain mentally. Rather, the solution will turn on the conditions under which our fellows in the semantic community accept our assertions.

The sceptical paradox, as Kripke has elaborated it, is that there is no fact of the matter as to what our words mean. There is nothing that can distinguish one word from another as the *correct* one; the notions of normativity and correspondence to facts are subject to paradox. So Kripke introduces a criterion of meaning and communication that he claims is Wittgenstein's answer to this paradox. It is a *sceptical* solution because, according to Kripke, Wittgenstein accepts the paradox, and tries to solve it without denying that it is true.

According to Kripke, in brief, what gives our assertions meaning is that other language speakers accept what we say (Kripke 1982: 77):

> All that is needed to legitimize assertions that someone means something is that there be roughly specifiable circumstances under which they are legitimately assertible, and the game of asserting them has a role in our lives. No supposition that 'facts correspond' to those assertions is needed.

Now what Kripke argues is that the circumstances in question involve reference to the *community.* As we suggested above, Kripke reads Wittgenstein as claiming that no one by herself can determine meaning; there is no such thing as a *private* language, understood as a language whose content is specified by me and me alone — on pain of paradox. So Kripke reads Wittgenstein's private language argument as a set of remarks aimed at dislodging the idea that one can, for oneself, determine one's own language and understanding. Rather, as Kripke claims, Wittgenstein view about the nature of meaning, meant to solve the sceptical paradox, is that meaning is established by public criteria. The community with which we, as it were, play the language game that we play is that which determines what we mean by our words.

This, according to Kripke, is the force of the idea that a private language is not possible — to follow a rule privately is not coherent. This is because, as we suggested above, the very idea of following a rule privately introduces the problem of *appearing* to do so as opposed to actually doing so. The notion of following a rule is crucial to that of what determines meaning, and the concept of following a rule collapses if it is possible to *think* one is doing so, so we must appeal to something to block that possibility.

As Kripke sees it, reading Wittgenstein as defending what is sometimes known as 'the community view' has the desirable outcome of both facing the sceptical paradox and solving it in a way that renders Wittgenstein's text less obscure and more cohesive.[23] The defense is roughly as follows. Others in the community can *check* and *agree* or disagree with the things that I say. They accept what I say with respect to a criterion: that of whether what I say *agrees* with what they would say under similar circumstances. If they disagree, they might do so for (at least) two reasons: either what I am saying is produced by some random, non-rule governed criteria; or, it is mistake that all the same is based on the kind of rule-governed criteria they recognize. The latter can still gain us entry to the community as fellow communicators; the former cannot.

The big picture, as Kripke argues, is given in Wittgenstein's emphasis on the 'form of life;' that is, our utterances have a role to play, and are useful (have a utility) in a wider framework. *We* simply are not alone in our communicative enterprises; we participate in a form of life, one that, according to Kripke, is what Wittgenstein believes is the nature of meaning and understanding. Part of participating in that form of life involves *expectations* that others will behave as we do with their words; we can rely on them, we can predict what they will say (exceptions of course can occur), and above all, we can understand them. Someone who produces sums according to say, the 'quus' rule, is not in conformity with *our* form of life, though they may well be with another. But someone who claims to be adding, and not *quadding*, will be judged and accepted to be doing so, so long as the utterances agree or conform to what the community members do themselves.

Kripke stresses[24] that, as he reads Wittgenstein, there is no appeal to *shared concepts*; that is, we don't agree about addition because we all share the same concept. Rather, the primitive fact about our communicative life is that we simply *do* agree with each other, we do communicate, and our words play a role, and have a use, in the activities that we call language and communication. This is what grounds the solution to the sceptical paradox, because it meets the paradox head on and sidesteps it neatly, and in a classic Wittgensteinian way. If we really look at the way we communicate, what we notice is that our interactions with others meld together the elements of agreement, acceptance, prediction, expectation, and the like. This is what happens — if it didn't there would be no communication. So, as Kripke concludes, this is at the heart of Wittgenstein's solution to the sceptical paradox. To mean, and to understand, is to exhibit and perform moves that are in conformity with, and accepted by, the community. A form of life is at the basis of meaning.

Rules and Private Language: A Summary

Kripke's interpretation of Wittgenstein has probably generated more disagreement than his work on modal logic or the lectures that comprise *Naming and Necessity*.[25] So to summarize the issues that have been treated in this chapter we can briefly elucidate a line of argument in contrast to Kripke's view, to indicate the shape of the broader picture.[26]

As some have noted, Kripke seems to read 'private' to mean individual, and 'individual' is opposed to 'public' — in the sense of one vs. many, alone vs. in company, solitary vs. social.[27] It's not clear that Kripke *argues* for this reading, and there may be another, more plausible one. One way to contrast the interpretations might be to say that Kripke might be correct in his claim that sensation-word examples — as in the private language argument — are but one specific case of a more general problem, but it is not clear that this supports the conclusion that the community is what determines meaning.

An opposing view is that Wittgenstein does not appear to take the issue of a community as seriously as Kripke seems to attribute to him in his interpretation. The textual situation is undoubtedly subtle. Wittgenstein does emphasize that language is an activity that takes place among those wishing to communicate, and that the context is important. But Wittgenstein could plausibly (more naturally?) be read as not taking the problem to be that of countering a picture that might otherwise appear desirable to us, by stressing the nature of the community and a community-based determination of meaning, in order to oppose a 'tempting' solitary, individualist, private determination. Rather, Wittgenstein might well be read as more interested in battling the inner mentalistic picture of meaning, and how it runs aground if we look at what grasping or understanding really consists of — and that, on this kind of view, is rule-following, carrying as it does a normative component. Wittgenstein seems to be claiming that nothing hidden or inner could have that normative component, because in a strictly private language, following a rule and *thinking that you were* would be the same — and that isn't normativity. The private language argument would be, on this reading, a strong way of illustrating Wittgenstein's explicit project.

Disagreement with Kripke could fall and, of course, has fallen[28] squarely on his reading of 'private;' he thinks it is to be understood in opposition to 'social.' Another view is that it could be understood along the lines of Wittgenstein's professed target: the hidden, the inner, the introspectively accessible, the mentalistic.[29] Any conception of meaning along these lines would undercut normativity, and Wittgenstein's investigation is meant to show that normativity is a key concept in language, meaning, and communication.

There is also a wider disagreement. The critical literature contains a number of claims against the view that Wittgenstein raises a sceptical paradox, and a sceptical solution, the way Kripke reads him, with various commentators citing different reasons for their rejection of Kripke's analysis.[30] So there is an ongoing dispute in the literature as to whether passage that Kripke cites as evidence (*PI* 201), in fact supports a statement of a paradox concerning the impossibility of meaning anything by our words. Another view might well be that it is squarely in line with Wittgenstein's project: what he notes is that rule-following *can*, on the face of it, exhibit ambiguity. But in thinking that 'every course of action can be made out to accord with a rule' (and so, *no* course of action can), what we are doing is falling into a temptation to see rule-following as an entity that shadows our actions, like the bad conception of meaning is taken to 'shadow' or 'be associated with' our words, and thus taking that ambiguity as something it is not. Instead (*PI* 199):

> To obey a rule, to make a report, to give an order, to play a game of chess, are *customs* (uses, institutions).

> To understand a sentence means to understand a language. To understand a language means to be master of a technique.

The opposing view reads Wittgenstein as tying the nature of meaning to rule-following, and uses the rule-following considerations to undercut the inner state or process conception of meaning. There is, that is, some strong reason to believe that Wittgenstein is arguing for guarding against the temptation to see rule-following as the very thing that he is claiming meaning is not. Rule-following only seems to exhibit ambiguity if we insist on seeing it as an entity that must be grasped and intended in our use of words. Rather, what we must see is that rule-following carries its own brand of normativity with it, and that it is *this* that meaning consists of. We follow rules in grasping, conveying, and understanding meaning; and this is evident, Wittgenstein claims, in that we are able to grasp, convey, and understand meaning time and time again, in future activities, without jeopardizing communication. To understand means to do so on indefinitely many future occasions, successfully. If this is indeed what Wittgenstein means by rule-following, then it may not so clear that the rule-following considerations support a radical scepticism about meaning, as Kripke argues.

Conclusion

In fact, however, Kripke's interpretation of Wittgenstein ultimately stands as some of the strongest evidence of the major and central influence Kripke has had on the past 40 years of philosophy of mind and philosophy of language. If the mark of a great philosopher is the amount of attention — agreement and disagreement — that his work generates, its originality, and its influence, then, without doubt, Saul Kripke is a great philosopher. His published works are absolutely foundational in the field. Everything he has ever published has been discussed, lauded, criticized, pored over, and analyzed. His work is the subject of classes and seminars; conference talks; books, journal articles, and commentaries. His work on Wittgenstein, modal logic, possible worlds semantics, and the host of points he makes in *Naming and Necessity* are probably the most influential ideas in the latter part of 20th century philosophy. Kripke recently retired from Princeton University, and anticipation in the philosophical community for further work runs high. Kripke could never write another word of philosophy, and yet retain the reputation of greatest living philosopher, but it is to be hoped that he will furnish the philosophical community with more of his ideas in the years to come.

ENDNOTES

[1] See, for instance, Frongia and McGuinness (1990). Page numbers here refer to the book published in 1982; an earlier version was published as a lengthy article. We must forgo detailed comment on his views regarding other minds, published in the appendix to (1982). Kripke there extends the sceptical paradox he claims to have detected in Wittgenstein's remarks on rule-following to the question of other minds, and offers a reading of Wittgenstein on this issue that builds on the earlier one.

[2] But see Fogelin (1976), Chapter XII, for a similar view.

[3] It is difficult to offer an exposition of Wittgenstein that completely extrudes one's own views. See Preti (2002) for a more complete elaboration of the interpretation of Wittgenstein suggested in contrast to Kripke's here.

[4] See Monk (1990).

[5] See Sluga and Stern (1996) for a helpful and concise introduction to Wittgenstein's life and work.

[6] See Frongia and McGuinness (1990) for an overview.

[7] See (among many others): Anscombe (1984); Baker and Hacker (1984; 1980); Fogelin (1976); McGinn (1984).

[8] Wittgenstein sometimes talks about 'a *queer* process' in this context (*PI* 196).

McGinn (1984) explains Wittgenstein's anti-mentalistic views about meaning by linking them to the historical conception of mental content defended by empiricists, classical to contemporary. The contrast is illuminating, whether or not the interpretation is correct. In my view, we might see Wittgenstein as making an implicit criticism of empiricist views by way of an act/object distinction.

[9] One way to tie together the points Wittgenstein makes in the rule-following considerations and the private language argument is by way of an emphasis on the concept of normativity, as we will see. And one way to contrast Kripke's interpretation of Wittgenstein with another possible view is to claim that although Wittgenstein places heavy emphasis on the the notion of the *application of a sign*, the issue with respect to normativity that emerges is not the same as the one that Kripke claims reveals the sceptical paradox. More on this below (see endnote 21).

[10] There is disagreement over this. See, for instance, the contrast in Blackburn (1983), Coates (1986), Gert (1986), McGinn (1984), and Tait (1986), who accept the conception I am defending here, and (for instance), Boghossian (1989), who doesn't.

[11] A critical, and as yet undefined, concept. See below.

[12] But see Goldfarb (1985: 473, ftnt 5):

.....in general, [Kripke] does claim the stance of an exegete. He says, "The present work is intended to expound my understanding of Wittgenstein's position" (30/1), and he talks of not wanting to "abandon the role of advocate and expositor." (146).

[13] Kripke (1982: 8).

[14] Kripke claims that the sceptical paradox has a metaphysical aspect and an epistemological aspect. The metaphysical aspect is the doubt shed on whether there is any

fact of the matter as to meaning *plus* and not *quus*. The epistemological aspect of the paradox is the doubt shed on whether one has any justification for claiming that one means *plus* and not *quus*. The two are related in that if there were any fact of the matter, it would act as justification.

[15] This may sound more like an assertion on my part than is strictly justified here. I make good on it below.

[16] Commentators have not hesitated to note the affinity between Kripke's sceptical paradox and Goodman's so-called 'grue' paradox. See, for instance, McGinn (1984).

[17] Some commentators disagree. See McGinn (1984).

[18] We will be brief: Kripke spends more time on this option because of what he notes is a fairly widespread interpretation of Wittgenstein as defending a dispositional analysis of meaning; and the dispositional analysis *per se*.

[19] There is a strong temptation to say that, if nothing else, these candidates fail from the start because Wittgenstein's main target is any sort of inner mental state analysis of meaning or understanding; qualitative conscious states and dispositions both qualify as just the kind of thing Wittgenstein takes as his target.

[20] Kripke (1982; 62-90).

[21] This should not be misunderstood. It's not that Kripke ignores normativity with respect to meaning. But what Kripke does is emphasize a certain normative relation between meaning and *symbols,* discovering therein, he argues, the sceptical paradox. Kripke finds scepticism to arise with respect to what we can call *constancy*: whether there is any fact of the matter that constitutes the meaning of a given symbol in its use over time; whether, that is, my present use conforms to past intentions in respect of that sign (and on what basis, if so).

This scepticism may or may not arise with respect to content *itself,* independently of how it attaches to symbols. The view that reads Wittgenstein as making important claims about understanding, rules, and private language by way of normativity takes the latter notion to be one that should be understood more widely than Kripke does (in his focus on the meaning of a symbol over time), and places a different, and possibly critical, emphasis on it. See Preti (2002) for the extended argument.

[22] Whether Frege's theory of sense, or Russell's more

directly referential view. Both *involve* a mental state or process: for Frege, grasp of a (mind and language independent) sense, associated with our words. For Russell, what he called *acquaintance* is, in effect, a grasping relation between the mind, universals, and (as he claimed) sense-data. Wittgenstein was concerned to jettison the whole picture that these theories supported.

[23] Kripke gives a strong briefing on what he thinks is the structure of *PI* in (1982: 78-90).

[24] Kripke (1982: 90).

[25] See, for instance, Baker and Hacker (1984: vii):
...it was evident that Kripke's interpretations flew flagrantly against Wittgenstein's manifest intentions in these important passages, misconstruing their meaning, mis-identifying their target, and misrepresenting their thrust.

See also the essays in Holtzman and Leich (1981).

[26] See Preti (2002).

[27] See, for instance, McGinn (1984); also the discussion in Llewelyn (1986), and Loar (1984).

[28] See McGinn (1984).

[29] See McGinn (1984). I extend the point in another direction here.

[30] See the bibliography in Frongia and McGuinness (1990), and the lengthy discussion in McGinn (1984), as well as the critical comments of (among others) Gert (1986), Loar (1985), Tait (1986), Winch (1984), and Wright (1984).

Bibliography

Works of Saul Kripke

"A Completeness Theorem in Modal Logic," *Journal of Symbolic Logic* 24 (**1959**): 1-14.

"The Undecidability of Monadic Modal Quantification Theory," *Zeitschrift fur Mathematische Logik und Grundlagen der Mathematik* (8), **1962**.

"Semantical Analysis of Modal Logic (I)," *Zeitschrift fur Mathematische Logik und Grundlagen der Mathematik* (**1963**): 67-93.

"Semantical Considerations on Modal Logic," *Acta Philosophica Fennica* 16 (**1963a**): 83-94.

"Semantical Analysis of Modal Logic (II)," in *Theory of Models*, ed. by J. Addison, Leon Henkin, and Alfred Tarski (Amsterdam: North Holland, **1965**): 206-220

"Semantical Analysis of Intuitionistic Logic I" in *Formal Systems and Recursive Functions: Proceedings of the Eighth Logic Colloquium* (Oxford 1963). Edited by J. N. Crossley and M. Dummett. Amsterdam: North-Holland, **1965**.

"Identity and Necessity," in *Identity and Individuation*, ed. M. Munitz, (New York: New York University Press), **1971**: 135-64.

"Naming and Necessity," in *Semantics of Natural Language*, ed. D. Davidson and G. Harmon (Dordrecht: Reidel, 1972): 253-355. Page numbers in text refer to the monograph *Naming and Necessity* (Cambridge, Mass.: Harvard University Press), **1980**.

"Speaker's Reference and Semantic Reference," in *Definite Descriptions: A Reader*, ed. Gary Ostertag (Cambridge, Mass.: MIT Press, **1998**): 225-56.

"A Puzzle About Belief," in *Meaning and Use*, ed. A. Margalit (Dordrecht: Reidel, **1979**): 239-83.

"Outline of a Theory of Truth," *Journal of Philosophy* (72) #19: November 6, **1975**: 690-716.

"Is there a Problem about Substitutional Quantification?" in *Truth and Meaning*, ed. John McDowell and Gareth Evans (Oxford: Clarendon Press): 325-419.

Wittgenstein: On Rules and Private Language (Cambridge, Mass.: Harvard University Press), **1982**.

Review of Three Papers by Kit Fine, *Journal of Symbolic Logic,* Vol. 50, No. 4, (December, **1985**): 1083-93.

"From the Church-Turing Thesis to the First-Order Algorithm Theorem," in *Proceedings of the 15th Annual IEEE Symposium on Logic in Computer Science* (LICS **2000**).

Secondary Bibliography

Anscombe, G.E.M. 1984. "Wittgenstein on Rules and Private Language," *Ethics* (95): 342-52.

Baker, G., and P.M.S. Hacker, 1980. *Wittgenstein: Understanding and Meaning; An Analytical Commentary on the Philosophical Investigations, Volume I.* Oxford: Basil Blackwell.

Baker, G., and P.M.S. Hacker., 1984. *Scepticism, Rules, and Language.* Oxford: Basil Blackwell.

Becker, O. 1930. "Zur Logik der Modalitäten," *Jarbuch fur Philosophie und Phaenomenologische Forschung*, Vol. 11: 497-548.

Blackburn, S., 1984. "The Individual Strikes Back", *Synthese*: 281-2.

Boghossian, P. , 1989. "The Rule-Following Considerations," *Mind* Vol. 98, #392 (October): 507-49.

Burge, T., 1979. "Individualism and the Mental," *Midwest Studies in Philosophy, Vol. IV.,* ed. P. French, T.E. Uehling, Jr., and H.K. Wettstein (Minneapolis: University of Minnesota Press): 73-121.

Burge, T., 1979. "Sinning Against Frege," *The Philosophical Review* (Vol. 88, July, 1979): 398-432.

Burge, T., 1986. "Individualism and Psychology," *The Philosophical Review* (95) (1): 3-46.

Branch, T., 1977. "New Frontiers in American Philosophy," *New York Times Magazine:* 12-67.

Carnap, R., 1947. *Meaning and Necessity.* Chicago: University of Chicago Press.

Coates, P., 1986. "Kripke's Sceptical Paradox: Normativeness and Meaning," *Mind* (95): 77-80.

Dummett, M., 1981. *Frege: Philosophy of Language.* Cambridge, Mass.: Harvard University Press.

Feys, R. 1937. "Les logiques nouvelles des modalités," *Revue Neoscholastique de Philosophie,* Vol. 40 (pp. 517-33); Vol. 41 (1938: pp. 217-52).

Feys, R., 1965. *Modal Logics.* Paris: Gauthier-Villars.

Fetzer, J., and Humphreys, P., eds., 2000. *The New Theory of Reference: Kripke, Marcus and its Origins.* Dordrecht: Reidel.

Fodor, J., 1987. *Psychosemantics.* Cambridge, Mass.: MIT Press.

Fogelin, R.1976. *Wittgenstein.* London: Routledge and Kegan Paul.

Frege, G., 1879. "Begriffsschrift," in Geach and Black, 1980.

Frege, G., 1980. *The Philosophical and Mathematical Correspondence.* edited by Brian McGuinness. Oxford: Basil Blackwell.

Frongia, G., and Brian McGuinness, 1990. *Wittgenstein: A Bibliographical Guide.* Oxford: Basil Blackwell.

Geach., P. and Max Black, 1980. *Translations from the Philosophical Writings of Gottlob Frege,* 3rd Edition. Totowa, NJ: Barnes and Noble Press.

Gert, B., 1986. "Wittgenstein's Private Language Arguments," *Synthese* (68): 409-439.

Goldfarb, W., 1985. "Kripke on Wittgenstein on Rules," *The Journal of Philosophy* (Vol. 82, #9): 471-88.

Goodman, N. 1972. "The New Riddle of Induction," in *Problems and Projects* (Indianapolis: Bobbs-Merrill):371-88.

Hintikka, J., 1969. *Models for Modalities.* Dordrecht: Reidel.

Holt, J., 1995. "Whose Idea is it Anyway? A Philosopher's Feud," *Lingua Franca.*

Holtzman, S., and C. Leitch,, 1981. *Wittgenstein: to Follow a Rule.* London: Routledge and Kegan Paul.

Hughes, G.E. and M.J.Cresswell, 1968. *An Introduction to Modal Logic,* London: Methuen.

Kanger, S., 1957. *Provability in Logic.* Stockholm: Almqvist and Wiksell, 1957.

Lewis, C. I., 1918. *A Survey of Mathematical Logic.* Berkeley: University of California Press.

Lewis, C.I., and Langford, C.H., 1932. *Symbolic Logic.* New York and London: Century; 2nd ed., New York: Dover, 1959.

Lewis, D.K., 1968. "Counterpart Theory and Quantified Modal Logic," *Journal of Philosophy,* Vol. 65: 113-126.

Llewelyn, J. 1986. "Following and Not Following Wittgenstein," *Inquiry* (29): 363-70.

Loar, B., 1985. "Wittgenstein on Rules and Private Language," (review), *Nous* (Vol. 19, Issue 2): 273-280.

Marcus, R.B., 1993. *Modalities.* New York: Oxford University Press.

McDowell, J. 1984. "Wittgenstein on Following a Rule," *Synthese.*

McGinn, C., 1984. *Wittgenstein on Meaning.* Oxford: Basil Blackwell.

McGinn, C., 1989. *Mental Content.* Oxford: Basil Blackwell.

Monk, R., 1990. Ludwig Wittgenstein: The Duty of Genius. London: Penguin.

Neale, Stephen, 2001. "No Plagiarism Here: The Originality of Saul Kripke," Review of Fetzer and Humphreys (2000), *Times Literary Supplement,* #5106, February 9, 2001: 12-13.

Peirce, C. 1930-58. *Collected Papers,* ed. Hartshorne, Weiss, and Burks. Cambridge, Mass.: Harvard University Press.

Putnam, H., 1973. "Meaning and Reference," *Journal of Philosophy* LXX (19): 699-771.

Preti, C., 1992. "Opacity, Belief, and Analyticity," *Philosophical Studies* 66 (3): 297-306.

Preti, C., 1995. "Externalism and Analyticity," *Philosophical Studies*. 79 (3): 213-36.

Preti, C., 2000. "Belief and Desire Under the Elms," *Protosociology*, Vol. 14 (October 2000): 144-157.

Preti, C., 2002. "Normativity and Meaning: Kripke's Sceptical Paradox Reconsidered," *The Philosophical Forum* (Vol. XXXIII, No. 1): 39-62.

Quine, W.V.O., 196. *From A Logical Point of View.* Cambridge, Mass.: Cambridge University Press.

Quine, W.V.O., 1976. *The Ways of Paradox and Other Essays.* 2nd edition, Cambridge, Mass.: Harvard University Press.

Russell, B., 1918. "The Philosophy of Logical Atomism,' in *Logic and Knowledge* (ed. Robert Marsh). London: Unwin/Hyman: 175-281.

Russell, B., 1919. "Descriptions," in *Introduction to Mathematical Philosophy* (New York: Touchstone Books): 167-80.

Salmon, N. and Scott Soames, 1988. *Propositions and Attitudes.* Oxford: Oxford University Press.

Searle, J. R., 1958. "Proper Names," *Mind* (67): 166-73.

Sluga, H., 1996. *A Cambridge Companion to Wittgenstein.* Cambridge: Cambridge University Press.

Smart, J.J.C., 1959. "Sensations and Brain Processes," *The Philosophical Review*, LXVIII: 141-56.

Sobociński, B. 1953. "Note on a modal system of Feys-Von Wright," *The Journal of Computing Systems,* Vol. 1: 171-178.

Tait, W.W., 1986. "Wittgenstein and the Sceptical Paradoxes," *The Journal of Philosophy(* Vol. 83, #9): 475-88.

Van Heijenoort, J. (ed)., 1967. *From Frege to Godel: A Source Book in Mathematical Logic, 1879-1931.* Cambridge, Mass.: Harvard University Press.

Von Wright, G.,1951. *An Essay in Modal Logic.* North Holland Publishing Company.

Whitehead, A.N., and Russell, B.A.W., 1910-1913. *Principia Mathematica* (Cambridge: Cambridge University Press), 3 vols. First edition 1910-1913, Second edition 1923-1927.

Winch, P., 1984. "Facts and Super-Facts," *The Philosophical Quarterly* (Vol. 33. No. 133): 398-404

Wittgenstein, L., 1922. *Tractatus Logico-Philosophicus.* London: Routledge and Kegan Paul.

Wittgenstein, L.,1953. *Philosophical Investigations*. Oxford: Basil Blackwell.

Wright, C., 1984. "Kripke's Account of the Argument Against Private Language," *The Journal of Philosophy* (Vol. 81, Issue 12): 759-78.